Books are to be returned on or before
the last date below.

TEL. 0151 231 4022
LIVERPOOL L2 2ER

LIVERPOOL
JOHN MOORES UNIVERSITY

Personality Disorder

LIVERPOOL
JOHN MOORES UNIVERSITY
AVRIL ROBARTS LRC
TITHEBARN STREET
LIVERPOOL L2 2ER
TEL. 0151 231 4022

D0280572

Forensic Focus Series

This series, edited by Gwen Adshead, takes the field of Forensic Psychotherapy as its focal point, offering a forum for the presentation of theoretical and clinical issues. It embraces such influential neighbouring disciplines as language, law, literature, criminology, ethics and philosophy, as well as psychiatry and psychology, its established progenitors. Gwen Adshead is Consultant Forensic Psychotherapist and Lecturer in Forensic Psychotherapy at Broadmoor Hospital.

Secure Care for Women
An Integrated Approach
Anne Aiyegbusi and Ray Travers
Forensic Focus 16
ISBN 1 85302 775 8

Ethical Issues in Forensic Mental Health Research
Edited by Gwen Adshead and Chris Brown
Forensic Focus 21
ISBN 1 84310 032 0

Neither Bad Nor Mad
The Competing Discourses of Psychiatry, Law and Politics
Deidre N. Greig
Forensic Focus 20
ISBN 1 84310 006 1

Psychiatric Assessment
Pre and Post Admission
Valerie Anne Brown
Forensic Focus 8
ISBN 1 85302 575 5

Psychiatric Aspects of Justification, Excuse and Mitigation in Anglo-American Criminal Law
Alec Buchanan
Forensic Focus 17
ISBN 1 85302 797 9

A Practical Guide to Forensic Psychotherapy
Edited by Estela V. Welldon and Cleo Van Velsen
Forewords by Dr Fiona Caldicott DBE and Helena Kennedy QC
Forensic Focus 3
ISBN 1 85302 389 2

Forensic Focus 23

Personality Disorder
Temperament Or Trauma?

An account of an emancipatory research study carried out
by service users diagnosed with personality disorder

Heather Castillo

Jessica Kingsley Publishers
London and Philadelphia

All rights reserved. No part of this publication may be reproduced in any material form (including photocopying or storing it in any medium by electronic means and whether or not transiently or incidentally to some other use of this publication) without the written permission of the copyright owner except in accordance with the provisions of the Copyright, Designs and Patents Act 1988 or under the terms of a licence issued by the Copyright Licensing Agency Ltd, 90 Tottenham Court Road, London, England W1P 9HE. Applications for the copyright owner's written permission to reproduce any part of this publication should be adressed to the publisher.
Warning: The doing of an unauthorised act in relation to a copyright work may result in both a civil claim for damages and criminal prosecution.

The right of Heather Castillo to be identified as author of this work has been asserted by her in accordance with the Copyright, Designs and Patents Act 1988.

First published in the United Kingdom in 2003
by Jessica Kingsley Publishers Ltd
116 Pentonville Road
London N1 9JB, England
and
325 Chestnut Street
Philadelphia, PA 19106, USA

www.jkp.com

Copyright © Heather Castillo 2003

Library of Congress Cataloging in Publication Data

Castillo, Heather.
Personality disorder: temperament or trauma? / Heather Castillo.
p. ; cm -- (Forensic focus; 23)
Includes bibliographical references and index.
ISBN 1-84310-053-3
1. Personality disorders. 2. Temperament. 3. Psychic trauma. I. Title. II. Series
[DNLM: 1. Personality Disorders--therapy. WM 190 C352p 2003]
RC554. C37 2003
616.85'8--dc21

2002035295

British Library Cataloguing in Publication Data
A CIP catalogue record for this book is available from the British Library

ISBN 1 84310 053 3

Printed and Bound in Great Britain by
Athenaeum Press, Gateshead, Tyne and Wear

Contents

Dedication   6

Acknowledgements   7

1   Dreaming of a Better Way   9

2   A Historical Perspective   13

3   The Disliked Patient   19

4   Personality Development   23

5   Complex Post Traumatic Syndrome   27

6   Treatability   31

7   Is Suffering an Illness?   37

8   Getting Our Act Together   41

9   The Task   51

10 Demographics and Themes   55

11 What Personality Disorder Means to Us   69

12 Experiences   99

13 The Moral Career of the Client   127

14 The Diagnostic Straightjacket   135

15 Spreading the Word   147

16 New Beginnings   155

References   165

Index   171

For John and Jamie,
my wonderful sons

Acknowledgements

I would like to say a very special thank you to our user researchers, Karen, Raine Adams, Julian Rooke and Linda Kelly, for their wonderful dedication, sometimes in the face of very great personal difficulties. Great thanks to Lesley Allen whose letter to the Health Authority in 1997 was an important catalyst and who continues to campaign tirelessly. Thank you to Kathy Warner, who contributed so much to this study. To Debbie Tallis, whose letter to *The Guardian* in 1997 added significant impetus. To my friend and our director, Andy Whittaker, who, yet again, intuitively encouraged me in a piece of work that might have been considered an uncomfortable proposition. To Clive White and the trustees of Colchester Mind, who supported me in this endeavour, which turned out to be far more time consuming than first anticipated. Thank you to the managers and consultants of the local Mental Health Trust for their co-operation regarding work with their clients for a study which could potentially lay bare a deal of disaffection. To our Trust link, Judy Acland, who was just that, someone to trust, because she is a therapist who had already helped many of our group. Thank you to all those who provided academic papers for our study, especially Dr Neil Coxhead for the information about trauma and for his continued support. Thank you to Dr Gwen Adshead for her very helpful editorial advice. To Reg McKenna, my computer guru, and to Helen Gilburt, for their invaluable help with charts and tables. And to my husband Alex, long-suffering proofreader and sounding board.

Great thanks are also due to Anglia Polytechnic University, which provided the funding for this study, and our academic supervisors, Dr Nicola Morant, former researcher from the Henderson Hospital, for help with training and her knowledge of methodology, and to Professor Shulamit Ramon. Anyone who knows Shula, has read her books, or who has had the good fortune to be taught by her, will not need to ask why she is such an inspiration.

Finally, my greatest thanks go to the 50 service users whose lives, experiences and thoughts are revealed in this study.

CHAPTER 1

Dreaming of a Better Way

For too long a time, for half a century in fact, psychiatry tried to interpret the mind merely as a mechanism, and consequently the therapy of mental disease merely in terms of technique. I believe this dream has been dreamt out. What now begins to loom on the horizon are not the sketches of a psychologised medicine but rather those of a humanised psychiatry.

Viktor Frankl (1962, p.136)

When I look around me at the world of psychiatric diagnoses that has evolved I see a need for a fundamental questioning of its limitations. From where did these assumptions arise and what are their historical destinations? It seems fitting, therefore, to begin this search for meaning with the words of Viktor Frankl, a holocaust survivor. Some children survive their own quiet holocaust. What comes next, and how might children who are grown transcend such experiences?

This story is essentially a study carried out for and by service users with a Personality Disorder diagnosis I simply provided the window-dressing. The setting for our study is an established advocacy service run by Mind, based in an acute mental health unit adjacent to Colchester General Hospital. Many of the service users involved in this story were known to me as advocacy service manager. I had advocated for them for some years and there was a background of association and trust.

The American and European psychiatric diagnostic manuals refer to Personality Disorders as enduring patterns of behaviour that deviate markedly from the expectations of the individual's culture, and pervasive, inflexible deficits which are stable over time (DSM IV 1994; ICD 10 1992). This gives the service user little cause for any hope at all. It is a category which does not have much scientific credibility and it is a diagnosis which is often hidden from patients. Some journeys are embarked upon not simply out of fascination but rather they are impelled by a sense of urgency and injustice. During the 1990s a growing number of people with the Personality Disorder diagnosis sought advocacy support from the service in Colchester; however, our assistance in finding solutions to their problems was largely ineffective. Some had simply been denied mental health services, others had lost their children via child protection procedures, some had been sent to secure hospitals, others ended up in prison. What became clear was that they did not feel understood, and the responses they received tended to exacerbate their situation, frequently resulting in worsened behaviour. In February 1997 a service user from Cambridge published a story in *The Guardian* called 'A Criminal Waste of Life and Time'. This was in fact her premise, a criminal waste of five years of her life and of the service's time. Of her transfer to a secure hospital she said, 'It was the worst day of my life…I only knew that murderers and bad people went to places like Broadmoor. I did not realise that people labelled as self-harmers were put in such places.' (Tallis 1997) This brought about an awareness of the possibility of a national situation regarding this diagnosis, rather than it being merely a local concern. In July 1997 a consultant in public health for North Essex Health Authority published an article in *The Guardian* called 'Everyone's life has a price'. His suggestion that money could be saved by denying hospital admission to those with Personality Disorder prompted a local service user to write from hospital in Colchester stating, 'I am a victim of childhood sexual and ritual abuse. I am not yet a survivor. I don't see why I should be deprived of the care and expert counselling that I most definitely need. It was, after all, not me who carried out abuse on a minor. I am just trying to cope with the aftermath' (Allen 1997). There are two focal points highlighted above: the right to be in hospital, and the right not to be incarcerated in hospital. They appear to be in conflict but reflect that people in this category are at risk of not receiving the kind of care they need. This risk was, and continues to be, important enough to justify a public and publicised debate.

In July 1999 the Home Office issued policy proposals for managing dangerous people with Severe Personality Disorder, suggesting removal to special units, without deterioration in clinical state, if deemed potentially dangerous to the public (DoH 1999a). This seemed to cause fairly widespread fear amongst those with the diagnosis. The advocacy service began to hear from anxious service users who had at some time received the diagnosis or who had at one time assaulted another, no matter how minor the offence. Notwithstanding assurances regarding the small number proposed for indeterminate detention, and their historical dangerousness, many were not calmed. 'This is doing time for no crime'; 'It's the thin end of the wedge'. The impulse to form a local research group arose from a growing and shared sense of alienation amongst those who had attracted the label. One of our group wrote to Tony Blair to express her concerns about the proposals. She received a reply from Robert Furness at the Department of Health. He claimed, 'We have in hand a number of initiatives aimed at improving community services for vulnerable people with Personality Disorder'. He did not describe what these 'initiatives' would be.

By this time I had encountered a kind of inspiration from Professor Shulamit Ramon who taught me that service users had indeed carried out very credible research and service monitoring (Beeforth, Conlan and Grayley 1994; Rose et al. 1998). Shula's postmodern view of research gave me a taste of freedom and a sense of possibility (Ramon 2000). The now late Professor David Brandon brought his own unbounded ideas regarding the authentic power of service users' views (Brandon 1991). I was fortunate to be among the last students that he taught. David pointed out that, like a clock running backwards, a service had evolved from professional perspectives rather than the needs of the people. I began to see that, as a mental health advocate, by nature partisan and with a role to 'side with the client', I was placed in an ideal position to facilitate the voice, the views, and an account of the inner world of those who had attracted a diagnosis of Personality Disorder.

Together with my service user friends, I set out to seek some answers. Like a tightrope walker crossing a chasm, I proceeded with a certain naïvety and a certain optimism, and I believe this was probably the only way I had of keeping my balance during subsequent years. We began our investigations deep in the past.

CHAPTER 2

A Historical Perspective

A thing which has not been understood inevitably reappears, like an unlaid ghost, it cannot rest until the mystery has been resolved and the spell broken.

Sigmund Freud (1909, p.137)

Two hundred years ago, in 1801, the French psychiatrist, Pinel, spoke of 'manie sans delire', mania without delirium. Pinel defined what might now be called Dissocial Personality Disorder, and believed it was characterised by unexplained outbursts of rage and violence in the absence of impaired intellectual function or delusion. At that time delusions were regarded as a central factor of mental illness and Gelder, Gath and Mayou (1989) presume that this group also included those mentally ill patients who were not deluded, for example, those suffering from mania or mood disorder.

In 1835 a doctor at Bristol Infirmary, Pritchard, formulated a new term, Moral Insanity, defined as 'a morbid perversion of the natural feelings, affections, inclination, temper, habits, moral dispositions and natural impulses' (p.126). Pritchard considered that instances of moral insanity also included the melancholy and the unnaturally excited. The new classification again appeared to refer to both Personality Disorder and mood disorder.

Further classifications were suggested throughout the nineteenth century, including Monel's *Congenital Delinquency* in 1852, followed by *Degenerative Deviation, Moral Imbecility, Constitutional Inferiority* and *Moral Deficiency* (Gelder, Gath and Mayou 1989). Later in the century a recognition of mental illness without delusion occurred, and distinctions were drawn between schizophrenia and affective or mood disorders. The concept of moral insanity was consequently modified. In 1872 Lambroso spoke of the 'unborn criminal' and in 1884 Henry Maudsley wrote 'It is not our business, and it is not in our power, to explain psychologically the origins and nature of these depraved instincts, it is sufficient to establish their existence as facts of observation' (p.ix). Maudsley described one patient as having 'no capacity for true moral feeling' and conceived of 'a form of mental alienation which has so much the look of vice or crime that many people regard it as an unfounded medical intervention' (1885, p.127). However, the concept was here to stay and remained a forerunner to Koch and Kraepelin's investigations into 'Psychopathic States'. By 1891, the German doctor, Koch, introduced the term 'Psychopathic Inferiority'. Kraepelin (1905) was to replace 'inferiority' with 'personality'. He defined the Psychopathic Personality as falling into seven types: excitable, unstable, eccentric, liars, swindlers, antisocial and quarrelsome.

At the turn of the last century, the existing Lunacy Act did not certify 'socially dangerous' people because 'Insanity is necessarily a disorder of intelligence, that it means delusion, or it means intellectual disorder, or intellectual defect'. Therefore, the 1904 Royal Commission on the Care and Control of the Feeble Minded proposed that the 'moral imbecile' should become an additional category of patient to whom care and control should be extended. This category was defined as 'Persons who from an early age display some mental defect, coupled with strong vicious or criminal propensities on which punishment has little or no different effect'. The 'Moral Defective' then became a category incorporated into the Mental Deficiency Act 1913.

In 1923 Schneider, another German psychiatrist, was to extend the classification of Psychopathy, to include ten subclassifications incorporating not only those who caused suffering to others but also those causing suffering to themselves and not necessarily others. He included among them markedly depressive and insecure characters. If there already existed confusion concerning the barriers between behaviour, mood and illness, Schneider's theory was to introduce two clearly different meanings for the term. It now included not just dissocial characteristics but a much wider meaning regarding personality abnormalities of all types.

In 1941, Cleckley coined the phrase 'the mask of sanity' and confusion regarding nomenclature continued with Sir David Henderson's book *Psychopathic States* (1939, p.128). Henderson began by defining psychopaths as people who 'Throughout their lives, or from a comparatively early age, have exhibited disorders of conduct of an anti-social or asocial nature, usually of a recurrent or episodic type which in many instances have proved difficult to influence by methods of social, penal or medical care or for whom we have no adequate provision of a preventative or curative nature'. However, Henderson went on to broaden his definition to include three groups of psychopaths: aggressive, inadequate and creative. Examples of the latter suggested by Henderson were Joan of Arc and T.E. Lawrence. His classifications also included those prone to suicide, drug and alcohol abuse, pathological lying, hypochondria, instability and sensitivity.

Shorter (1997) examined the fact that the Second World War presented psychiatric challenges which were different from insanity but that only terms such as Psychopathic Personality were available for understanding them. He suggests that this demand for new systems in classification multiplied psychiatric diagnoses, which became included in DSM 1 (1952), thus lowering the threshold and increasing the patient base.

Borderline Personality Disorder was a concept devised around the 1950s to describe patients who were considered to be on the borderline between neurosis and psychosis. Many clinicians disputed this borderline and the concept evolved into a Personality Disorder. Those with Personality Disorder are defined in DSM IV (1994, p.459), the American Diagnostic and Statistical Manual of Mental Disorders, as 'These impulsive people [who] make recurrent suicide threats or attempts. Affectively unstable, they often show intense inappropriate anger. They feel empty and bored and they frantically try to avoid abandonment. They feel uncertain about who they are and lack the ability to maintain interpersonal relationships.' ICD10 (1992, p.205), the European Classification of Mental and Behavioural Disorders, defines 'Emotionally Unstable Borderline Type' as 'Disturbed self-image, aims and preferences. Chronic emptiness, intense unstable relationships and self-destructive behaviour'.

By the 1950s it was considered that the 1913 Mental Deficiency Act legislated for an insufficiently homogenous group. Concern was expressed about how to deal with 'moral defectives of higher intelligence'. This saw the first legal definition of Psychopathy within legislation, in the 1959 Mental Health Act. It is this definition that is largely retained within the current Act. Antisocial or Dissocial Personality Disorder is a clinical diagnosis often used interchangeably with Psychopathic Disorder which is defined in the Mental Health Act 1983 as 'A persistent disorder or disability of mind (whether or not including significant impairment of intelligence) which results in abnormally aggressive or seriously irresponsible conduct on the part of the person concerned'. Response to treatment is required before an individual can be detained under the Act. Many problems have arisen regarding this fact. Finding an instrument in law which gives reasoned consideration to the question of treatability is difficult (Clift 1999). In Scotland this has been very widely interpreted in recent case law where the definition of treatability was defined as an alleviation of the deterioration of symptoms, rather than treating the disorder itself (Reid vs Secretary of State for Scotland 1999). A major concern within Government remains one of public safety and containment. This is reflected in the Department of Health and Home Office Consultation Document (DoH 1999a, p.5) and its proposal to detain people in this category without limit of time. 'Some have a criminal history but are not convicted of any current offence. Most are not admitted to hospital because they are assessed as unlikely to benefit from the sorts of treatments that are available.' Here emerges the newest subcategorisation of Personality Disorder. Appearing initially as an imprecise but 'useful' clinical term called Severe Personality Disorder (Kernberg 1984; Norton and Smith 1994; Tyrer 1988), it is now described in government documents as 'Dangerous Severe Personality Disorder'.

Therefore, the modern concept of Personality Disorder is represented by two connected notions: either that the personality abnormality causes problems to self and/or others, or that behaviour is so antisocial as to be dangerous to society. The concern of the medical profession remains a history of the definition and classification of surface manifestations, and, theoretically, ten subclassifications of Personality Disorder exist today. They are defined in ICD 10, and a definition table of these classifications, together with their transatlantic comparisons from DSM IV, is shown as Table 2.1.

Gelder, Gath and Mayou (1989, p.129) ask us to consider that 'Human beings resist precise measurement and, unlike the phenomena of disease, abnormal individuals cannot be classified neatly into the manner of clinical diagnosis'. Dr David Fainman of the Henderson Hospital suggests that 'behind the label of Personality Disorder there is a personality, behind which is a person. We have struggled with what these labels mean for years. All of us have personalities and ten per cent of us in the general population are considered to have a Personality Disorder' (Tyrer and Stein 1993, p.42).

The classification of Personality Disorder continues to generate a kind of moral panic in society, although its clinical definitions range from the most timid to the most dangerous among us. The diagnosis is characterised by confusion and lack of agreement. Where understanding is required, fear has emerged.

Table 2.1 ICD and DSM IV subclassifications

ICD 10		DSM IV		
Code	Description	Code	Description	Cluster
F60.0	**Paranoid** – excessive sensitivity, suspiciousness and hostile perceptions of others' motives and behaviour, excessive self-importance and reference (≥3 criteria)	301.00	**Paranoid** – distrust and suspiciousness of others' motives/actions as deliberately demeaning, threatening or untrustworthy(≥4 criteria)	A. Odd Eccentric
F60.1	**Schizoid** – social and affectional withdrawal, preference for fantasy, solitary activities and introspection. Limited capacity to express feelings and experience pleasure (≥3 criteria)	301.20	**Schizoid** – detachment from social relationships, restricted range of expression and emotions interpersonally, reduced desire for experience (≥4 criteria)	
F21	**Schizotypal** – (coded under schizophrenia, schizotypal and delusional disorders)	301.22	**Schizotypal** – social and interpersonal deficits, discomfort and reduced capacity for close relationships, cognitive or perceptual distortions and behavioural eccentricities (≥5 criteria)	
F60.2	**Dissocial** – disregard for social obligations, callous unconcern for others, low frustration tolerance, tendency to blame others, deviant social behaviour (>3 criteria)	301.70	**Antisocial** – disregard for and violation of rights of others since age 15, conduct disorder before age 15 (≥3 criteria)	B. Dramatic Emotional
F60.30	**Emotionally unstable, impulsive type** – emotional instability, poor impulse control, inability to control anger, plan ahead or think before acting, quarrelsome (≥3 criteria)		**(Subsumed under 'Borderline')**	
F60.31	**Emotionally unstable, borderline type** – disturbed self-image, aims and preferences, chronic emptiness, intense unstable relationships, self-destructive behaviour (≥3 criteria)	301.83	**Borderline** – unstable interpersonal relationships, self-image, affects and impulsivity (≥5 criteria)	

F60.4	**Histrionic** – shallow labile affect, self-dramatisation, egocentric, inconsiderate of others, continuous need for appreciation (≥3 criteria)	301.50	**Histrionic** – Excessive emotionality and attention seeking in various contexts (≥5 criteria)	
	Not specifically coded for. Can be classified under other specific personality disorders (F60.8)	301.81	**Narcissistic** – grandiose fantasy or behaviour, need for admiration, lack of empathy (≥5 criteria)	
F60.5	**Anankastic** – doubt, perfectionism, excessive conscientiousness, caution, stubbornness, rigidity, preoccupation with details (≥3 criteria)	301.40	**Obsessive–compulsive** – pervasive preoccupation with orderliness, perfectionism, mental and interpersonal control at expense of flexibility, openness and efficiency (≥5 criteria)	C. Anxious Fearful
F60.6	**Anxious (avoidant)** – persistent feelings of tension, insecurity and inferiority. Continuous yearning to be accepted and liked, hypersensitive to rejection, restricted personal attachments, social avoidance due to exaggerated risk (≥3 criteria)	301.82	**Avoidant** – pervasive social inhibition, feelings of inadequacy, hypersensitivity to negative evaluation (≥4 criteria)	
F60.7	**Dependent** – a passive reliance on others for decisions, fear of abandonment, helplessness, incompetence, passive compliance	301.60	**Dependent** – excessive need to be taken care of, submissive and clinging behaviour, fears of separation (≥5 criteria)	
F60.8	Other specific personality disorders – e.g. narcissistic, incompetence, passive compliance (≥3 criteria)	301.9	Personality disorder not otherwise specified – e.g. passive aggressive personality disorder, depressive personality disorder	
F60.9	Personality disorder unspecified			

CHAPTER 3

The Disliked Patient

Personality Disorder appears to be an enduring pejorative judgement, rather than a clinical diagnosis.

Lewis and Appleby (1988, p.44)

In his analysis of secure provision Larry Gostin (1985) recognised the tendency for people diagnosed with Personality Disorder to be excluded from services or to receive inappropriate care in special hospitals or prison. Bell and McCann (1996, p.206) indicate attitudes still prevail that those diagnosed with Personality Disorder 'need to try harder because their behaviour is under control' or 'are not to be trusted and may attempt to kill themselves with medication' and 'have enduring patterns which may even worsen in therapy'. Grove (in Oldham 1994, p.1774) describes the challenge of trying to treat 'hateful patients', 'independent clingers', 'entitled dreamers', 'manipulative help rejecters' and 'self-destructive deniers'.

Lewis and Appleby (1988) report that untreatability is a widely held belief. In their study 'The Patients Psychiatrists Dislike', a random sample of 240 psychiatrists were assigned one of six case histories. Patients who had a previous history of Personality Disorder were seen as difficult, annoying, manipulative, attention seeking, in control of their suicidal urges and less deserving of care.

Dunn and Parry (1997, p.19) describe Borderline patients who repeatedly cut themselves, try to hang themselves or overdose. 'The staff are often stressed and deskilled, the psychiatrist is frustrated and irritated, and other clients are both traumatised and neglected as a result of obvious management problems which affect the units.' They were struck by the number of clients who generated a lot of chaos and stress in the mental health service: 'The person who keeps their appointments erratically in spite of repeatedly asking for crisis responses; the young woman who repeatedly presents at A & E with deliberate self-harm or suicide attempts.' These sorts of behaviours were characterised as 'Arousing negative feelings... This is not mental illness, it is attention seeking, or acting out, or behavioural, or badness... Often the psychiatrist feels torn between those who think this client should be in hospital and those staff who know that they do not have a coherent plan for treatment.' A secure setting, with a regime bounded by the Mental Health Act and Home Office Orders, may activate all an individual's despair and rage regarding authority. This can result in rebellion, self-harm, absconsions, and threatened or actual violence against patients and staff. Add substance misuse to any of the above situations and a truly compounded problem may result.

Bob Hinshelwood (1998, p.187), Professor of Psychoanalysis at Essex University, hypothesises that difficult patients create reactions in those who try to care for and treat them. He suggests this results in an emotional retreat on the part of staff into what he calls the 'scientific attitude'. This retreat causes 'scientific justification' which can blind staff to some aspects of the subjective experience of the patient. 'That blind-spot crucially feeds back directly into the patients' difficulties.' Hinshelwood believes this professional defence causes staff to lose sight of rich information about the complexity of relating which is right there in front of them.

Freud's difficult feelings are described in relation to a patient suffering from paranoid schizophrenia (Hinshelwood 1998). Here was 'a man for whom meaning itself has gone', suggesting a quality 'so distant from myself and from all that is human'. In this situation 'meaning' may disappear for both parties, and with it the humanitarian and subjective interest of the professional. Families in this situation may feel they must remove the family member with psychosis from a 'human' to a 'treatment' setting and the person may be seen as a troublesome object that only professionals can restore (Laing and Esterson 1964).

Hinshelwood's thesis is that those with Severe Personality Disorder pose an opposite situation. Rather than the distancing effect of incomprehensible meaning, they offer 'a relationship too intensely suffused with human feelings – usually very unpleasant ones'. He characterises such patients as operating 'predominantly in a world of feelings' and they 'directly and deliberately, although unconsciously, interfere with our feelings. We feel intruded upon and manipulated – and indeed, *we feel.*'

Experiencing this as a kind of abuse of time, help and care, the professional may fail and be in danger of being overwhelmed. Rather than the depersonalisation of the schizophrenic into an object, someone with a Personality Disorder diagnosis may find the condemnatory label extended to 'bad' not 'mad', and the perception of them becomes a compounding of strong moral judgement. Professional debates regarding Personality Disorder have extended beyond the clinical arena. The role of the media in shaping opinion inflamed the public response to events in the early 1990s surrounding psychiatric patients such as Ben Silcot and Christopher Clunis (Ramon 1998). The latter part of the decade has seen a shift of media focus and public fears to such cases as Robin Lane, Tony Gamble and Michael Stone (Gillan & Campbell 1998). Brutal murder and Personality Disorder are now featured synonymously in the press.

A hundred years ago schizophrenia was not considered treatable and was often categorised together with some of the most degenerative of physical conditions, such as severe syphilis. The AIDS epidemic has moved beyond vilification. Advances in knowledge not only improve the treatment of human conditions, they can also change the emotional response to them.

CHAPTER 4

Personality Development

My mother loves me.
I feel good.
I feel good because she loves me.

I am good because I feel good.
I feel good because I am good.
My mother loves me because I am good.

My mother does not love me.
I feel bad.
I feel bad because she does not love me.

I am bad because I feel bad.
I feel bad because I am bad.
I am bad because she does not love me.

She does not love me because I am bad.

R.D. Laing (1971, p.9)

The Freudian concept of personality development acknowledges the role of the unconscious and presumes that early experience is the cause of later emotion and behaviour. Melanie Klein (1946) suggested that the mother's breast was a primal object in early external relations, an object which could manifest not only nurture, love, life and safety for the infant but also greed, hate and persecutory feelings if withdrawn. Klein's premise, that object relations exist from early life, the mother's breast being the first object which for the child becomes split into good (gratifying) and bad (frustrating), proposes that this splitting results in a severance of love and hate. An interplay occurs between introjection and projection and, to escape persecutory feelings and depressive pain, an individual may blame or idealise, demonise or fantasise about external 'objects' (people, things or situations).

During the 1930s and 40s studies occurred in both the US and the UK which began to highlight the impact of early childhood experiences on personality development. These experiences included prolonged institutional care, war, homelessness, and loss or frequent change of the mother figure during early life (Bender and Yarnell 1941; Burlingham and Freud [Anna] 1942; Hargreaves 1949). In 1950, English psychoanalyst John Bowlby began to develop his Attachment Theory. The studies of the previous decade left him in no doubt that inadequate maternal care in childhood and separation of children from those they know and love had an adverse effect on personality development. Bowlby began to question what features of experience are responsible for distress. If the child forms ties to the mother primarily because it is the mother who feeds the child, the personal relationship, or 'dependency', of child on mother might be viewed as secondary. Bowlby challenged this theory. He considered that the Kleinian emphasis on food and orality did not match his experience of children. Instead of starting with the adult, expressing thoughts and feelings years later, and attempting to trace origins retrospectively, Bowlby began by observing children who had experienced early trauma and attempted to build a theory of personality development from this information.

An individual tries to maintain proximity to another clearly identified person who is perceived as being able to cope better with the world and is expected to give care, comfort and security. This encourages us to value and continue relationships. Bowlby recognised that this 'attachment' behaviour is emphasised in childhood but also continues throughout life. A child or adult who has attachment to someone is strongly disposed to stay near and seek contact with that individual, especially in times of threat and emergency. He expanded the theory of 'Separation Anxiety' by pointing out that both psychoanalysts and psychiatrists had made an unexamined assumption that fear is aroused in mentally healthy individuals only by obviously dangerous or painful situations. He observed that increased risk also carries a signal, for example threats to abandon a child as a means of control, or parental threat of suicide. He suggested that this might also result in increased arousal, not just in terms of fear, but also intense anger, especially in older children or adolescents (Bowlby 1988).

Verrier (1993) proposes that Attachment Theory and Separation Anxiety have huge significance in terms of the biological mother, and suggests we neglect the fact that the unborn child has already accumulated experience and achieved bonding during the 40 weeks prior to birth. She sees this as a continuum of physiological, psychological and spiritual events which, for those children who are adopted, can result in a loss which is indelibly imprinted on the unconscious mind as a 'primal wound'. Bowlby also challenged traditional psychoanalytic theory in terms of the model of developmental stages a child is expected to pass through. Rather, he proposed that the child has an array of potential pathways for personality development, some mentally healthy, some not. Bowlby considered that these pathways might be determined by the environment the child meets along the way.

The dialectical theory of self-development assumes that a 'sense of self' develops through the perception of oneself in another person's mind. An infant builds up a viable sense of self from the repeated internalisation of the mother's processed image of the child's thoughts and feelings. This provides containment. Not only does the mother, or close care giver, interpret the baby's physical expressions, she also gives back to the child a manageable interpretation of what is being communicated. Peter Fonagy (1997), Freud Memorial Professor of the Anna Freud Centre in London, suggests that an absence, or distortion, of this early mirroring experience can lead to a desperate search on the part of the child to find alternative ways of containing psychological experience. This may develop into destructive physical expression, either towards self or others. A child who has not received recognised, but modified, images of behaviour and emotional states may have trouble in differentiating reality from fantasy, and physical from psychic reality. This suggests a tendency in later life, to cope with thoughts and feelings through physical action. *Do it either to my body or their body.* Not being able to feel themself from within, that individual is forced to find a sense of self from outside by treating themself as an object or by getting others to react to them. This results in experience of self in a more authentic, if very limited, way and the need for re-enactment to augment the incomplete representation of self which has been achieved.

At puberty this factor may become critical because the body changes in shape and function in a way which signifies a far greater change in identity for those whose sense of self has been impaired. This has relevance for the development of existential anxieties and anorexia in adolescents, where the body shape may literally be felt to represent aspects of the personality. A feeling of well-being and relative integrity can sometimes be achieved by cutting or self-starvation. Fonagy suggests this is because the mind is left feeling more contained or bounded, and belonging more to the self, as the body is sacrificed.

In his paper on 'Transgenerational Transmission of Holocaust Trauma', Fonagy (1999) outlines an attachment-theory based model of transgenerational trauma where the transmission of specific trauma ideas is shown to cross generations. Holocaust trauma may undermine parenting capacity in a survivor who may suffer depression and poor control of emotions, guilt and aggression.

This can impact on the infant–parent relationship when the frightened or frightening care giver cannot adequately mourn the 'murdered objects' of past experience. The objects are then recreated in the mind of the second-generation survivor at the cost of extinguishing an authentic sense of self. This telescoping of holocaust trauma through generations has caused Fonagy to conclude that much more needs to be learned about second-generation victims of unresolved trauma. Main, Kaplan and Cassidy (1985) also ask us to consider that an infant's behaviour may trigger flashbacks in a parent who has suffered from trauma.

Tenable psychodynamic theories exist, yet there appears to be little interchange between those trying to conceptualise personality development and clinicians who aim to understand and treat Personality Disorder. Even less interest has been manifest regarding what service users may have to say about themselves beyond sensationalist writing about multiple Personality Disorders such as *Sybil* (Schreiber 1973).

CHAPTER 5

Complex Post Traumatic Syndrome

I have been told I was a perfect baby and a very bubbly child ... From 7 or 8 years old I
suddenly changed...I was always alone...I did not go to school... I was disruptive...
I began to have fits and blackouts and memory loss. No one could understand why my
personality had changed so suddenly...no one but myself and my older brother.

Case study – Ainscough and Toon (1996, p.19)

In his practice manual for treating Post Traumatic Stress Disorder
Meichenbaum (1994) discovered that 70 per cent of those diagnosed with Borderline Personality Disorder are survivors of childhood sexual abuse. Joseph,
Yule and Williams (1997) observe that there is accumulating evidence for an
additional form of more Complex Post Traumatic Stress Disorder. Felicity de
Zueleta (1999, p.238), examining the disorder from an attachment perspective,
claims to be attempting 'to provide mental health care workers with a way of
making sense of some of the individual's terrifying, soul destroying experiences and their destructive, even though often defensive behaviours'. Zueleta
suggests a reframing of the category into Complex Attachment Disorder.

Herman (1992) also reviewed evidence for this and concluded that
'Unsystemised but extensive empirical support exists for the concept of a
post-traumatic syndrome in survivors of prolonged, repeated victimisation'.
Herman considered that this may sometimes co-exist with Post Traumatic
Stress Disorder but, whether it did or not, it extended beyond it. 'The syndrome
is characterised by enduring personality change and high risk for repeated
harm, either self-inflicted, or at the hands of others.' Herman also proposed
that: 'Traumatised people are frequently misdiagnosed and mistreated in the
mental health system. Because of the number and complexity of their
symptoms, their treatment is often fragmented and incomplete.' He observed
that: 'Because of their characteristic difficulties with close relationships, they
are vulnerable to become re-victimised by caregivers. They may become

engaged in ongoing, destructive interactions, in which the medical system replicates the behaviour of the abusive family.'

Dunn and Parry (1997) also recognise that those with this diagnosis tend to relate to mental health services as they would to parents, enacting early abusive developmental roles. This has caused mental health services in Hull and Holderness to adopt a formulation which attempts to listen to the client's earlier abusive experiences within the system and aims to achieve collective ownership of the problem before treatment options are discussed. An innovative formulation has also been created by one therapist in Colchester which aims, as a primary action, to focus on the diagnosis in terms of damaged personality, thereby shifting attention to what happened to that person in earlier life rather than compounding the guilt and suffering of feeling inherently bad (Acland 1999). Such interventions, where they have arisen, seem to have been grasped intuitively by experienced front-line workers in a hectic climate where sufficient training and knowledge do not exist. Such formulations are not always consistent with the wider service area.

Acknowledgement of the profound effects of trauma was set in motion during the First World War when men experienced shell-shock. Many common soldiers were shot for desertion, but when officers of proven character began to be afflicted this provoked a crisis in Victorian psychiatric theory (Stone 1985). Psychiatry rediscovered the impact of trauma in the early 1970s and the diagnosis of Post Traumatic Stress Disorder was included in DSM III. Today DSM IV includes, within the criteria for possible diagnosis, combat victims, survivors of disaster, rape, kidnap or hostage, and children who have been victims of sexual and other abuse. ICD 10 includes survivors of combat, disaster, accident, torture, terrorism, rape and witnessing violent death. Abuse in childhood is not included within the possible criteria.

In 1994 the American Psychiatric Association, aware of research into Post Traumatic Stress Disorder, included an additional category in DSM IV, under Table 9.2 for Disorders of Extreme Stress Not Otherwise Specified, 'DESNOS'. This acknowledged that trauma affected a whole range of core psychological functions including arousal, consciousness, somatisation, character changes and meaning. In ICD 10 this is included as F.62 (pp.208–210) 'Enduring Personality Change, not Attributable to Brain Damage and Disease'. Emphasising personality change after severe psychiatric illness, it also encompasses catastrophic experience. Examples include concentration camp experiences, torture, disasters and prolonged exposure to life-threatening circumstances, for example, hostage situations and prolonged captivity with an imminent possibility of being killed. Again, childhood trauma is not explicitly stated.

Nemiah (1995, p.4), in his study of early trauma, considers 'since psychiatry has started to organise psychological problems in a diagnostic system that is based purely on their surface manifestations, it has, as a profession, increasingly lost interest in the workings of the mind and the mystery of medicine'. The inclusion of Post Traumatic Stress as a category of psychiatric disorder is judged by the American psychiatrist Bessel Van der Kolk (1996) to open the way to scientific investigation into the nature of human suffering. He believes that this begins to correct the emphasis on disorders as 'things' and focuses attention within the context of personal histories and environments, and brings us back to living people, their experiences and the meaning they give to those experiences.

Herman and Van der Kolk (1987), in their work with incest victims and Vietnam veterans, discovered that trauma, especially prolonged trauma from care givers, had a profound effect on personality development and the development of Borderline Personality Disorder. They concur with Fonagy (1997) that behaviour manifestations of self-mutilation, revictimisation, victimising others, dissociative disorders, substance abuse and eating disorders, are an effort to regain internal equilibrium. Van der Kolk (1996, p.3) has characterised this condition as 'the black hole of trauma' and has described Post Traumatic Stress as a failure of time to heal all wounds. For some, there is an inability to integrate the traumatic experience. He points out that there is a very complex interrelationship between traumas, neglect, environmental chaos and attachment patterns, and that clinicians fail to pay attention to the effects of early trauma or to perceive the patterns of reliving, warding-off reminders or repetitive re-exposure to situations reminiscent of trauma.

Kingsley Norton and Bridget Dolan (1995, p.319) examine 'acting-out' and the institutional response in terms of an unconscious emotional conflict which causes a sense of impulse and immediacy. This impulse, often performed as a scenario of great fidelity, involves a rehearsed and carefully scripted but unconscious activity and is performed in an effort to replace, with action, the inability to recall trauma. 'A typical example is the Personality Disordered inpatient who self-mutilates rather than seeking support and speaking about distress.' Eliciting strong emotional reactions from those around, this fixed behaviour may result in expressions which are professionally questionable and a therapeutic stalemate. Norton and Dolan consider custodial psychiatric institutions, involving a limited repertoire of surveillance, sedation and seclusion, to provide the kind of immediate response from the environment that an 'acting-out' patient is requiring. Restoration of control may reassure staff and provide short-term relief from pain and insecurity for the patient, but does not explore motive and consequences or help someone to achieve psychological maturity by remembering the emotional conflict. Van der Kolk (1996, p.204) suggests that clinicians often become rescuers, victims or victimisers because 'these are patients who are force-fed, thrown into seclusion, medicated against their will, and/or transferred without warning'. Sometimes they are simply discharged with optimistic care plans which are a paper exercise masking a truer therapeutic pessimism.

Van der Kolk (1996) has also measured the physiological effects of trauma by examining responses to specific stimuli. He discovered significant increases in heart rate, skin conductance and blood flow, increased hormone release, decreased serotonin activity and increased opiate release often associated with dissociative states. He suggested that problems with arousal and stimulus response may account for the high incidence of the diagnosis of Attention Deficit Hyperactivity Disorder in traumatised children. His discoveries also have implications for research claims in relation to symptomatic improvements for pharmacological treatments of Personality Disorders including low-dose neuroleptics for perceptual distortions, tricyclic and serotonin uptake anti-depressants for depressive symptomatology, mood stabilisers for impulse control and benzodiazepines for anxiety (Oldham 1994).

Simply uncovering memories of trauma is considered by Van der Kolk (1996) to have little therapeutic benefit. These memories need to be reconstructed in a way that is meaningful to the person. He also advocates helping that person to become attached to other experiences of feeling safe, understood, strong and capable. Being able to empathise with and help fellow sufferers is cited as potentially healing. A sense of safety from therapeutic massage is also found to help many women whose bodies had been violated. One illustrative example describes a woman suffering from nightmares, all treatments, including pharmacological, proving ineffective until she moved to a house which reminded her of the apartment of her loving aunt from childhood. She felt safe.

CHAPTER 6

Treatability

When the issue of causation becomes a legitimate area of investigation, one is inevitably confronted with issues of man's inhumanity to man, with carelessness and callousness, with abrogation of responsibility, with manipulation, and with failures to protect. In short, the study of trauma confronts one with the best and worst in human nature, and is bound to provoke intense personal reactions in the people involved.

Bessel Van der Kolk (1996, p.6)

In the early 1980s a speaker at a conference about cognitive behavioural approaches did not explicitly state the topic of his paper within the title because he feared being criticised as too radical or even heretical, because 'Personality Disorder was not a legitimate topic for behavioural research' (Pretzer 1994, p.257). Studies carried out during the 1980s about the effects of Personality Disorder on the cognitive treatment of other disorders, such as severe bulimia and social phobia, produced discouraging results (Giles 1985; Turner 1987). Roth and Fonagy (1997) note that most clinical trials for major depressive disorders have tended to exclude those with Personality Disorder. Those which have included such patients suggest poorer outcomes when there is a diagnosis of Personality Disorder.

However, in the late 1950s an uncontrolled study was carried out in which 42 patients were treated with psychodynamic psychotherapy. Predating the development of current diagnostic categories, clinical descriptions suggest the majority met the criteria for Borderline Personality Disorder. The approach was a blend of psychoanalysis, and expressive and supportive psychotherapy. Adopting a practical approach, analysis was rarely carried out in a pure form and included a significant degree of ego building. Follow-up data available for 27 of the sample showed a good long-term result for 11 and partial resolution for 7. The higher the ego strength the better the quality of interpersonal relationship and the more positive the outcome. Low ego strength was augmented with hospitalisation where necessary (Roth and Fonagy 1997).

Pretzer (1994) outlines a number of inconclusive and contradictory studies of the use of Cognitive Behavioural Therapy which have included Personality Disordered patients. Some showed that those who persisted through a full course of treatment responded well. Those studies which produced encouraging results tended to use a more flexible approach, tailored to the needs and characteristics of the individual.

During the 1990s Anthony Ryle (1997) pioneered the development of Cognitive Analytic Therapy (CAT) for Borderline Personality Disorder. This is an integrative approach using cognitive behaviour and psychodynamic therapy. Here the therapist also acts as a teacher or an enabler. Ryle recognised the value of the psychoanalytic concepts of Transference and Counter-transference, not just as a way of identifying shifting patterns encountered in treatment but also as a method of recognition and classification which could be used as a treatment tool. Ryle considered the diagnosis to be an 'unsatisfactory' one but felt it was currently 'irreplaceable'. He has attempted to go some way to address the discontinuity and variability of DSM IV and ICD 10 diagnoses by developing a model which overcomes some of these defects and tries to measure the degree of integration of the self. This gives the client the beginnings of a self-reflective way of integrating unavailable, dissociative parts of the self.

The internalisation of depriving and abusive care givers results in a narrow or distorted range of what Ryle calls 'reciprocal roles.' Pairs of reciprocal roles involve variations on the 'parent-derived role', the way we experience parenting and may later parent ourselves, and 'child-derived roles', the way we receive and respond to parenting. Examples of pair sets might include Abuser/Abused, Neglecting/Deprived, Controlling/Rebellious or Rejecting/Rejected. CAT therapists establish which aspect of the personality is maintaining dissociation and which particular contrasting self-state, or reciprocal role, the client uses to respond. Initial mapping of self-states is carried out collaboratively between therapist and client. This is a dialogic, active, problem-solving process which attempts to change destructive behaviour. Session numbers may extend from 16 to 24 and a good outcome would include internalisation of the therapeutic relationship, enabling the client thereafter to become their own therapist.

Parallel transatlantic studies by Marsha Linehan (1999) have resulted in Dialectical Behaviour Therapy (DBT) which has been developed specifically to treat Borderline Personality Disorder. Linehan considers that the disorder is the result of an emotionally vulnerable individual growing up in what she terms the 'invalidating environment'. Such an individual has an autonomic nervous system which reacts excessively to low levels of stress and takes longer to return to normal when stress is removed. The role of the DBT therapist is that of a teacher. Acceptance and validation are primary tools. The therapist will include frequent and sympathetic acknowledgement of an individual's suffering and sense of desperation, will believe that patients are doing the best they can and want to improve, will adopt a matter-of-fact attitude towards dysfunctional behaviour, will encourage an equal partnership with mutual commitment and goal setting, and will work to teach emotion-regulation skills and increased interpersonal effectiveness. Linehan, Oldman and Silk (1995) claim that the best treatment you can provide for someone with Borderline Personality Disorder is a consistent and caring professional relationship. Linehan's (1999) research provides the most widely known controlled outcome studies for the treatment of Personality Disorder. In the *National Service Framework for Mental Health* (DoH 1999b), issued in October 1999 the government has included Dialectical Behaviour Therapy and acknowledges its particular effectiveness in treating those who self-harm.

Co-existence of Personality Disorders with Axis I disorders is reportedly very high. Co-morbidity within Personality Disorders has also been identified. Antisocial Personality Disorder is frequently diagnosed in people with Borderline Personality Disorder (Roth and Fonagy 1997). Patients diagnosed with Dissocial Personality Disorder are considered by some psychoanalytic writers to have a basically Borderline personality structure (Ryle 1990). The subcategories of Personality Disorder are not mutually exclusive. With the investigation of causation, links are implied. Yet the development of psychological treatments has tended to be almost exclusively for Borderline Personality Disorder.

The case that breakthroughs in integrative approaches may have implications for the treatment of Dissocial Personality Disorder is possibly an unpopular one. Confronted with the worst in human nature, the current emphasis appears to be, not on engagement, but on detention without limit of time (DoH 1999a). How difficult is it for us to accept the membership of all within the human race? In her memoirs of Auschwitz, the French opera singer Fania Fenelon (1997) recognised that her fellows had changed, they had discovered a little something about the human race which they had not known before, and it was not good news. But she persisted in her refusal to call the perpetrators inhuman. The tragedy was that they were human. In February 1993 a two-and-a-half-year-old boy, called Jamie Bulger, was murdered. He was injured in a way that was difficult to accept or understand. This caused national grief and bitterness. Jamie's killers, two ten-year-old boys, were placed in detention. Lesser known facts are that Robert Thompson was one of seven children in a single-parent family, who habitually roamed the streets with little or no parental control. Jon Venables's family had been monitored by social workers for three years and he was a victim of violence (Britton 1998). Recent debate about whether they should have been released on reaching adulthood is more truly a debate about the right to rehabilitation, the need for punishment as a deterrent, and perpetration as a moral agent. Is the individual a perpetrator of crime, or a victim of severe Personality Disorder and a projection of society's ills? Crimes may be so horrific that it is not within the psychological gift of a society to acknowledge the possibility of rehabilitation.

Dr Bob Johnson, co-founder of the James Naylor Foundation, a charity devoted to the understanding and support of those diagnosed with Personality Disorder, considers that the question of untreatability is appalling. 'If you're a doctor you have a contract with your clients and customers and that's to try and treat. It doesn't say cure it says try and treat. We have here legislation on psychiatric practice that psychiatry endorses. I think we should set out to cure every harmed child' (Johnson 2000, p.40). Bob Johnson is a consultant psychiatrist who worked for five years in Parkhurst Prison treating those considered to have Dangerous Severe Personality Disorder. The thought-provoking nature of his work prompted the BBC to feature it in a *Panorama* programme called 'Predators' (Johnson 1999a). Johnson (1999b, p.4) considers that violence is always irrational, that it is an infantile response, a learned disease and a curable disease. He proposes that punishment is irrational and that it is also infantile. 'Every living process has an intent. If they can communicate it to you, you may begin to understand it, if they can't it doesn't mean that they have not got one' (p.7). At Parkhurst, Johnson increased his skills in recognising non-verbal behaviour and came to understand that human beings operate by consent and that consent is related to intent.

> I want to describe to you the process which I believe is going on and which I see in every psychiatric consultation I do. It is particularly useful when helping people who are cutting themselves or cutting other people or burning themselves or in other ways being violent inwards or outwards...
> Every dangerous individual has had an even more dangerous childhood. The child is growing up, hopefully it grows up smoothly. In some cases something terrible happens...so the child shuts the lid on the box. Inside the box is a terror... IF YOU WANT TO LIVE DON'T OPEN THIS BOX.
> (Johnson 1999b, p.13)

During Johnson's time at Parkhurst the number of violent incidents decreased. In the first seven years there were 52, in the last two years there was one episode of violence.

The intention of these most dangerous, most violent, 'untreatable psycho-paths', the intent was to be sociable. The unit was closed on ideological grounds. Sometimes I think we live in a feudal society in which the barons at the top make the decisions, and serfs like me and you go about our business. If I was director of a prison service and I was concerned that there were too many instances of violence, I would be interested in a situation where violence seemed to be going down. (Johnson 1999b, p.8)

David Glasgow (1998), a former psychologist at Ashworth Special Hospital, has stated, 'At the heart of the hospital has always been a therapeutic vacuum'. More recently, Special Hospitals have begun to address questions of treatment versus security needs for those with Personality Disorder and are beginning to introduce psychotherapeutic, cognitive and creative therapies (Guy and Hume 1999; Storey and Dale 1998). Currently, new assessment and treatment tools are being piloted at Rampton Special Hospital and Whitemore Prison. It has been suggested that the prison service looks after some 30,000 people with Severe Personality Disorder (Morris 1999). The Royal College of Psychiatrists (1999, p.34) is now proposing that more research is needed 'that may ulti-mately suggest new interventions for both primary prevention in childhood and adult offenders with Personality Disorder'.

Grendon Underwood Therapeutic Prison attempts to move away from the pure containment stereotype of prison. Grendon is highly selective about which prisoners they will accept and considers they must be very motivated because the clinical impression is that you can work with people if they are willing. Grendon employs behavioural boundaries and cognitive elements which are evidence based and have produced a 10 to 15 per cent reduction in reoffending. Dr. Mark Morris, the clinical director, believes that Nigel Eastman (1999) is wrong to say the prison service can hold all of this category because some people so severely self-harm that it is inhumane to try to treat them in prison. One prisoner at Grendon describes a therapeutic community regime for dangerous, long-term offenders who are willing to work at issues concerning their behaviour and its roots. 'I have been given the time and space to work through and dismantle all the justifications and cognitive distortions I used to excuse not only the behaviour of those who abused me but also my own offending behaviour' (Anonymous 2001a, p.18). Achieving what is sometimes described as 'victim empathy', this prisoner discovered: 'I have learned to see others as people with feelings and rights of their own, and not just as bodies on which to take out frustration, anger or selfish gratification' (p.20).

Therapeutic Communities have achieved acknowledged successes in the treatment of Personality Disorder. One consideration is that the attributes of Personality Disorder are evidence that an individual is vulnerable because they are unable to maintain control over their actions. When cared for in forensic medical settings, this is compounded as the individual is being held under the Mental Health Act. Encouraging results have been achieved by the Henderson Hospital, a therapeutic community in Surrey. Espousing the theory that the individual needs to regain control, the Henderson has a flattened hierarchy and considers 'the community as doctor'. The traditional medical model, which puts the patient in a passive role, is avoided. Peer selection and peer treatment strategies allow residents major responsibility in the running of the community (Dolan, Evans and Wilson 1992). Whiteley (1980) recognises the Henderson as a treatment option for patients who do not respond well to orthodox psychiatric services but are able to deal with exposure to therapeutic confrontation, with their peers, as a learning situation. Although the Henderson is not an option which is open to current forensic patients, Whiteley also indicates that the strongest lobby of support has come from forensic psychiatrists who have conceived of the Henderson as an alternative to the secure unit for mentally disordered offenders.

Menzies, Dolan and Norton (1993) argue that it is a false economy to deny specialist treatment as this may result in the consumption of considerable amounts of psychiatric, social, probation and prison services in an unproductive way. Follow-up studies for 24 Henderson patients showed a saving of £12,700 per person, per year, meaning the cost of specialist treatment could be recouped in under two years. The Department of Health have now taken measures to ensure that the Henderson is centrally funded and have supported the opening of two additional communities, in Salford and South Birmingham, based on the Henderson model.

CHAPTER 7

Is Suffering an Illness?

Psychiatry and neurology are not sister sciences, both belonging to the super-ordinate class called medicine. Psychiatry stands in meta relation to neurology and to other branches of medicine. Neurology is concerned with certain parts of the human body and its functions... objects in their own right... Psychiatry is expressly concerned with signs as things pointing to objects.

Thomas Szasz (1961, p.64)

If mental illnesses are diseases, they are diseases of the brain, not the mind. If mental illnesses are names of behaviour, they are forms of behaviour, not diseases.

Szasz (1991, p.1574)

Are neuroses disorders or diseases? Formerly described as a disease of the nervous system, the post-Freudian concept presents neurosis as a personality or mental disturbance not due to any known neurological or organic dysfunction (Reber 1985). Indicating a causal role played by unconscious conflicts evoking anxiety, the social context surrounding and preceding the disorder also has relevance. It has been argued that deviance results from the culture and structure of society (Merton 1968). It is suggested that society needs deviancy, as a projection of its own 'shadow', in order to safeguard the well-being of the majority (Durkeim 1970). Szasz (1961) continues a compelling argument that an 'illness model' pathologises human behaviour, fails to assign personal responsibility for condition and action, and promotes stigma, helplessness and dependency.

Whether a diagnosis, disease or disorder, epidemiological studies are likely to show the indirect costs of neurosis to be very high. But in considering the need for psychiatric services, establishing a diagnosis is only the first step. A crucial stage concerns treatment and resource implications. Psychiatrists Bracken and Thomas (1998) also question whether issues of distress and alienation are the sole concern of psychiatry, or whether they are social and political

37

issues which demand cultural change. They suggest that this should not be turned into a clinical issue requiring treatment and management and that psychiatry should accept its limitations. With the acceptance that Aneurin Bevan's vision of comprehensive health care for all is not likely to be a future reality, comes the concept of rationing. Already experienced in this area (North Essex Health Authority 1997; Ooi 1997) no further in-patient treatment for Personality Disorder was amongst the proposals. With acute services claiming that 95 out of 233 in-patients in a six-month period, approximately 40 per cent, are likely to have some element of personality problem, this did not become a reality (Acland 1997). However, rationing is at risk of continuing subtly. Claims of untreatabilty and diagnostic confusions are unlikely to help. The impulse to challenge the biological, reductionist model of psychiatry has enormous positive implications for exploration and creativity in terms of understanding and healing. However, it also has overtones of exclusion and of reasons to offload challenging, intractable and 'undeserving' cases. Pathologising and stigmatising suffering may compound the situation, but great suffering requires a response, and resources are currently concentrated within the psychiatric area. The questions are who requires a response and what should that response be?

Coid (1989) considers that an alternative is to view Personality Disorder as a single category. Norton and McGauley (1998) suggest that clients could simply be given a diagnosis of Personality Disorder if they fitted the basic definition, whether or not criteria required in subcategories are achieved. It is argued that personality psychopathology should be conceptualised by dimension rather than category because the complexity of one individual cannot be adequately defined by diagnostic label (Oldham 1994). According to DSM IV (1994) and ICD 10 (1992), a number of criteria must be present in order to diagnose a disorder. A dimensional system might rather look at the degree of anxiety, depression, sociability and trust. Whether or not someone with this diagnosis has committed a crime is also a dimensional consideration. Government guidance for the care and protection of severely mentally ill people, *Building Bridges* (DoH 1995), emphasises dimensional criteria which focus not just on diagnosis, but also on disability, duration, safety, and the need for informal or formal care. The Dimension Table of severe mental illness from *Building Bridges* (Figure 1, Chapter 1), interestingly, also includes Personality Disorder among the diagnostic criteria. A dimensional system implies clinical and economic answers to questions of service eligibility and demarcation.

A dimensional concept does not, however, fully address the basic categorisation of such human difficulties into a definition consistent with their aetiology. What is in a name? Stigma is in a name. Fear is in a name. Strong moral judgement is in a name, explicitly so in the nineteenth century. Pseudo insight through terminology is in a name. Erroneous insight through terminology is in a name. The literature suggests newer approaches to understanding and working with trauma, and ways in which the personality may become more integrated. Is this diagnosis really irreplaceable? Complex Attachment Disorder has been suggested as a name. Why, instead of 'manipulative' or 'acting-out' behaviour, do we not acknowledge 'attachment-seeking behaviour'? Complex Post Traumatic Stress Disorder has been suggested as a name. DESNOS or Disorder of Extreme Stress has been suggested as a name. These redefinitions more clearly encompass cause and are more compatible with effective treatment models.

Yet knowledge, which has begun to crystallise during the last 50 years, appears to be impeded by a sense of futility and fear. The gulf between sufferer and healer remains largely unbridged. Our premise is that part of the answer lies with service users themselves and their ability to bring the focus back to living people by describing personal histories and feelings in their own words and by evaluating those experiences in their own terms. Little attention has been paid to the service users with this diagnosis and the meaning they give to their inner world. This study invites you within.

LIVERPOOL JOHN MOORES UNIVERSITY
LEARNING SERVICES

CHAPTER 8

Getting Our Act Together

The very idea that small groups of 'experts' can get together and set a research agenda for disability is fundamentally flawed... Disability research should not be seen as a set of technical, objective procedures carried out by experts but part of the struggle by disabled people to challenge the oppression they currently experience in their daily lives.

Mike Oliver (1992, p.102)

Our group of 18 service users, all of whom had received a diagnosis of Personality Disorder, met monthly throughout 1999. *Esprit de corps* came easily to this group. Why should this be? After all, many of them were considered 'difficult customers'. Solidarity against the world, perhaps? There were certain hallmarks connected to our group. It was always the same room we met in. Warm. Next to the smoking room. A bottomless supply of tea, coffee and biscuits. Group cohesiveness occurred initially during shared experiences over loss of children and deepened throughout the year with much exploration of early history, experience of the psychiatric system and common coping strategies. The group was always unstructured. It resisted structure and ambled its way through two hours on a Thursday afternoon. Yet much was discussed and much was achieved.

Evans and Fisher (1999) examine power-sharing and encourage practitioners to assist users in carrying out research. Here both user and non-user researchers have something to offer and something to gain. Our power-sharing endeavour began as we fell into familiar roles. The group would provide the living experience, the stories. I would listen. Since advocates glean their information not from reports or from other professionals but from users themselves, this was familiar territory to me. I would provide the academic papers, the diagnostic manuals and definitions and we would mull over both theory and life together.

A vital early group decision was whether members with a Borderline diagnosis would be willing to, and feel comfortable about, including those with a Dissocial diagnosis. This seemed an important ethical decision because it

41

might be considered that 'abused' and 'abuser' would be drawn into unwilling association. Identifying common issues of stigma, discrimination and early life events, the consensus of the group was in favour of inclusion. This sense of solidarity might best be illustrated by a meeting which took place between two service users at our monthly venue later in the year. They recounted for us a story which occurred ten years ago when both were in-patients in the same ward. One had made a serious attempt on the other's life, and could have strangled her had it not been for restraint by staff. This story was recounted and viewed by both participants, not dispassionately, but with great honesty and acknowledgement of loss of control resulting in extreme provocation on the one side and extreme intention to harm on the other. Yet both service users now became united in overriding common purpose.

Our research approach was emancipatory. Described by Paolo Freire (1970) in his book *Pedagogy of the Opressed* as an approach which challenges the validity of the privileged effectively analysing the underprivileged, here the research tools would be given to the people. The 'view from above' would be replaced with the 'view from below' or from *within*. Brown and Harris (1978), in their study *Social Origins of Depression*, focused debate within sociology, psychology and psychiatry on factors not encompassed by physical and biological sciences. *Life Events and Illness* (Brown and Harris 1989) presents a more substantive message about provoking agents and vulnerability factors in relation to the aetiology of illness and disorders. Employing a narrative approach (Heron 1981), nine group members began to produce stories in order to examine the relationship between life events and their disorders. Some began to keep journals, others to write poetry or letters.

We were fortunate to have two skilled supervisors from Anglia Polytechnic University. Our principal supervisor was Shulamit Ramon, Professor in interprofessional and social studies, and our second supervisor was Dr Nicola Morant, senior lecturer from the psychology department and former researcher at the Henderson Hospital. With the help of supervisors we set out to create an interview questionnaire that would employ a blend of qualitative and quantitative methods (see the questionnaire at the end of Chapter 8). This begins with a semi-structured interview in order to give primacy to the voice of service users in a way which would not constrain their expression. The quantitative component of the questionnaire consists of a fixed format including a series of demographic, tick-box questions about gender, ethnic origin, family, domicillary and employment situations. This helps to profile our sample. The group made suggestions about the types of diagnoses, experiences and support systems which should be included. They advised on the kind of wording which would make the questionnaire real and understandable to fellow service users. In order to achieve increased generalisability, the group aimed to interview 50 people in the area who had attracted a Personality Disorder diagnosis.

Some members of the group had expressed a desire to train as research interviewers. In July 1999 five service users embarked on a training programme developed for this purpose (see Personality Disorder Research Training Programme at the end of Chapter 8). The programme was launched with an introduction to our subject, the concept of research and our aims. Communication techniques in the form of listening and responding skills were an important part of training. It was vital that interviewers should be aware that, whilst they might share a common reality with respondents, the purpose of the interview was to facilitate the sharing of experiences by the interviewee. Distress might arise on the part of respondents. This could also cause distress to interviewers. Objective and subjective ways of dealing with distress were, therefore, also addressed. This section of the training involved three hours of role play.

Professor Ramon conducted a training session which enabled the user researchers to look more closely at issues of power. This began with a free association, or stream of consciousness, session where they were asked *'What does power mean to you?'* This facilitated an exploration of power issues which began with experiences of personal disempowerment and developed into a subtler awareness of the unequal power relationship between interviewer and interviewee, and researcher and professional. Emerging issues concerned new-found power, positive power and the democratisation of power.

Dr Morant created a training session which addressed integral research themes regarding good practice, confidentiality, ethical issues, and the types and uses of interviews. This contributed skills and began to demystify more fully the research process. A further training session invited members of a co-operative enquiry group from Cambridge to join us to speak about their experience of being users who are researching. Our interviewers were able to benefit from their experiences, their study being further progressed than our own. Our final session endeavoured to draw together the practical issues and skills needed to commence the interviews, and also included timetables, expenses, mutual support and a final role play of the whole research interview carried out by each researcher. A small pilot experiment was then conducted where interviewers tested out their skills by using each other as the first respondents. The questionnaire was found to be workable, to facilitate answers and to accumulate data. The pilot resulted in an expectation that the research interviews would last approximately one hour.

A research grant was made available by the university and it was agreed that researchers would receive a payment of £30 for each interview conducted and respondents would receive £10 for their participation. We were now ready to begin the more systematic phase of our research.

Personality Disorder Questionnaire

Introduction: Interviewer to tell interviewee a little about who they are, why they have become involved in helping with this research, what the research is about and to ask if they would like to receive a copy of the final results. Assure confidentiality and explain that the interviewee is free to stop the interview at any point or decline to answer particular questions. Ask permission to take notes during interview. (Please use separate sheet to transcribe answers.)

1) What does Personality Disorder mean to you?

2) How did you find out about your Personality Disorder diagnosis?

3) If you were given a free hand to describe what you consider to be your problems what would you say?

4) Would you please tell me what you think your strengths are?

5) Could you please talk about any implications you think the diagnosis has had for how you have been supported/treated?

6) Could you please talk through experiences of the various services you have had?

7) What would you like in an ideal world, or what would you really like to see happen to you and the services you are in contact with?

Gender:	Male	☐	Female	☐
Town			Ethnic origin	
Age:	18–20	☐	45–54	☐
	21–24	☐	55–64	☐
	25–34	☐	65–74	☐
	35–44	☐	75 and over	☐
Marital status:			Living with:	
	Single	☐	Alone	☐
	Married/living as	☐	Partner	☐
	Divorced/Separated	☐	Partner + children	☐
	Widowed	☐	Single parent	☐
	Other	☐	Parents	☐
			Others – shared	☐
Housing:			Employment status:	
	Own house/flat	☐	'Sick' and claiming benefits	
	Rented house/flat	☐	Unemployed	☐
	Supported accomm.	☐	Retired	☐
	Hospital	☐	Employed part-time	☐
	Prison	☐	Employed full-time	☐

LIVERPOOL
JOHN MOORES UNIVERSITY
AVRIL ROBARTS LRC
TITHEBARN STREET
LIVERPOOL L2 2ER
TEL. 0151 231 4022

Tick the following boxes, as applicable:

Please tick more than one box if applicable:

Diagnosis:	
Personality Disorder – Borderline	☐
Personality Disorder – Dissocial Psychopathic	☐
Personality Disorder – Other (Please write if you know)	☐
Schizophrenia	☐
Manic Depression	☐
Obsessive Compulsive Disorder	☐
Depression	☐
Anxiety	☐
Post Traumatic Stress Disorder	☐
Eating Disorder	☐
Other (Please write if you know)	☐
Don't know	☐

Have you experienced any of the following?:

[Please stress again that the interviewee may decline to answer questions]

Cutting	☐	Other types of self-harm	☐
Overdosing	☐	Suicide attempts	☐
Alcohol misuse	☐	Drug abuse	☐
Overwhelming anger	☐	Desire to hurt others	☐
Violence to others	☐	Destroying things	☐
Being exploited	☐	Exploiting others	☐
Hospitalisation	☐	'Sectioned'	☐
Juvenile convictions	☐	Adult convictions	☐
Rejection from Services	☐	Isolation	☐
Disassociated/separate	☐	Imprisonment	☐
Abandonment	☐	Relationship difficulties	☐
Loss of children	☐	Early sexual abuse	☐
Early violent abuse	☐	Early emotional abuse	☐
Later abuse	☐		

Have you ever experienced or received support from any of the following?
(Please tick the appropriate rating box):

	Very Helpful	Helpful	OK	Not Helpful	Harmful
Family					
Friends					
Church/Spiritual Beliefs					
Hospital					
Day Hospital					
Therapeutic Community					
Safe House/Crisis House					
Voluntary Centres					
Community Mental Health Team					
Criminal Justice Mental Health Team					
The Police					
Solicitor					
Armed Forces					
Supported Housing					
Medication					
Psychiatrist					
Psychtherapy/ Counsellor					
Nurse					
Occupational Therapist					
Mental Health Social Worker					
Child Protection Social Worker					
Advocate					
Accident and Emergency					
General Hospital					
GP					

What would you say are the things which have helped you most?

(1) _____

(2) _____

(3) _____

Is there anything else you would like to add at the end of this interview? (Please use extra sheet to transcribe, as necessary.)

[Say thank you, reassure again about confidentiality and ask the interviewee if they would like to receive a copy of the completed questionnaire.]

Personality Disorder Research Training Programme

Session 1   Friday 16 April 1999
2pm to 5pm – Group Room 1 – Abberton Day Hospital
Trainer – Heather Castillo
- About Personality Disorder
- A simple introduction to research
- The research to date
- Aims and objectives of our continued research

Session 2 – Wednesday 21 April 1999
2pm to 5pm – Group Room 1 – Abberton Day Hospital
Trainer – Heather Castillo
- Good interview experiences
- Listening and responding skills
- Good communication qualities for researchers
- Responding to distress

Session 3 – Friday 23 April 1999
2pm to 5pm – Group Room 1 – Abberton Day Hospital
Trainers – Professor Shula Ramon and Dr Nicola Morant
- Being a user researcher
- Relationships with professionals and the users you are interviewing
- The aims of research
- Why use interviews in research
- Types of interview – strengths and weaknesses
- Ethical issues, e.g. confidentiality
- Good practice in asking questions
- Practical issues

Session 4 – Friday 30 April 1999
2pm to 5pm – Group Room 1 – Abberton Day Hospital
Trainers – Lifecraft Cambridge – Rea and Mary, and Debbie Tallis
- Users as researchers

Session 5 – Friday 7 May 1999
2pm to 5pm – Group Room 1 – Abberton Day Hospital
Trainer – Heather Castillo
- The questionnaire
- The environment
- How to set up and interview
- Timetables
- Expenses
- Pairing researchers for mutual support
- Hopes and fears
- Final role play – each researcher to practise doing an interview/ questionnaire

CHAPTER 9

The Task

Human beings are like tea bags. You don't know your own strength until you get into hot water.

Bruce Laingen, Iranian hostage 1979–81

It is important to understand that the researchers (see Chapter 8) were not 'survivors' engaged in a retrospective study, but rather 'sufferers' struggling for emotional equilibrium while engaged in a research endeavour. Consequently, our study was fraught with questions regarding who might relapse next and ethical dilemmas regarding the stressful nature of our enquiry. Our five researchers reduced to four almost as soon as the training programme had begun. Two more would also be admitted to hospital during the course of the study. All four researchers negotiated very great personal difficulties during this time, yet all four continued to contribute to the study as soon as they were able. One said, 'If I give up hope on this, then there's nothing left'. Other group members experienced their own individual problems. They still came to join us each month. Some came from the hospital wards. Some came even when 'sectioned'. The commitment was breathtaking.

Once training and pilot work were completed, it was necessary to obtain ethical permission to carry out our study. We were invited to attend a meeting of the local Research Ethics Committee on a warm evening in May. One of the service user researchers accompanied me to the meeting. At the entrance she asked, 'Do you think I should cover my arms?' On reflection, she did not feel she should have to do so. Bearing the scars of years of self-harm, she sat with some dignity and answered questions articulately and with candour. However, we suspected that such a research proposal might prove an uncomfortable proposition for any research ethics committee. Our suspicions were confirmed, and it took over three months of negotiations before permission for the study was granted.

Most debate occurred around confidentiality. Our main interrogator pointed out with some insistence that, where early abuse was revealed, named perpetrators must be reported to Social Services authorities, no matter how far in the past this abuse had occurred. I saw the confidentiality of our study disappear before my eyes and envisioned prospective respondents refusing to participate. We were not to be moved on this point. This would place the responsibility for the abusers in society with the overwhelmed abused. The Chair came to our rescue and negotiated the use of the Mind confidentiality policy, which is a discretionary policy in relation to disclosure. This was acceptable to us. However, the committee's concerns persisted. In the questionnaire, we had listed '*violet* abuse' instead of '*violent* abuse', saying something about our credibility, or lack of it. Why were our questions so negative? Why were our aims so grandiose? A study like ours would be unlikely to change things. What did we want to change anyway?

This imposed 'time out' was experienced as a low point by participants. Frustrated and demoralised the group decided in early July that interviews should proceed without approval because it was feared that permission might never be granted. 'We are free citizens, so why do we need anyone's permission to speak to each other?' Professor Ramon was overseas, and others counselled caution and a warning that no one, including the university, would support us if things should go wrong. On her return Professor Ramon suggested that it was true that people were, of course, free citizens but that it was also very desirable to obtain ethical approval. We renewed our endeavours to do so whilst also launching the research on a self-selected basis, involving members of the group. In August 1999 ethical permission was received. By this time we had completed 14 interviews.

After permission was obtained, we followed the guidance of the ethics committee by contacting seven local consultant psychiatrists with details of our study and asked for suggested respondents. However, although the psychiatrists were very co-operative in other ways, causing no delays and not refusing access to any of their patients, they suggested very few respondents for the study – three in all. By late November we had completed 40 interviews. Respondents had been almost entirely accessed by the networking activities of the advocacy service and the group. Only two had refused to be interviewed. Such a high response rate might be viewed as a testament to the support service users were willing to give to other service users involved in research. Networking had given us snowball sampling which gave us well over thirty respondents. This method only caused difficulty on one occasion. One of our researchers approached a woman who had once been a fellow in-patient with similar symptoms. She made an assumption regarding diagnosis. This happened to be a correct assumption. However, the woman in question thought that a breach of confidentiality had been committed by the local Mental Health Trust and she was very distressed. Many assurances were offered that this was not the case. She had been given the participant information sheet and contacted our named Mental Health Trust supervisor who was able to rectify the situation to the client's satisfaction. It was of interest to us that the only overtly expressed opinion that service users should not be allowed to carry out such research came from someone who actually had the diagnosis. My perception was that she saw the user researcher in terms of her own disempowered status.

The voluntary sector rallied support in the last few weeks, helping us to access the remaining ten interviewees. Nineteen interviews were conducted in respondents' homes, eighteen in hospital, nine at the Mind social centre or nearby voluntary centres, and four responded by mail, including two who had moved out of the area recently – one from an out-of-area secure unit, and the fourth wrote from prison. All interviews carried out at home involved respondents well known to us. One exception to this was an interview conducted at home due to respondent choice and restrictions regarding mobility. The researcher shared that, although no direct personal threat had been made to her, she had been very frightened during the interview, and I was to ensure that no researcher was placed in such a situation again. By 20 December 1999 the last interview was carried out. The sample of 50 was now complete.

I was charged with the task of making a systematic comparison of the sum total of raw data collected from the questionnaires and journals. This was an undertaking that, on occasion, reduced me to tears, so moving were many of the stories. Almost all respondents said they would like a copy of the completed report. When asked if they would like a copy of their completed interview, 11 respondents requested this. One had something further to add, another wanted to change a particular line, not because of interviewer inaccuracy but because he wished to make his statement more explicit. This section of the sample confirmed that they considered the interview to be a true reflection of their responses. Six researchers from our group offered to carry out a further analysis of the findings by reading through the first draft and making comments on categorisations. Capturing the voice of the sample, the data collected from the group and the questionnaires had a quality of undeniability and yielded a vast quantity of service user perspectives. Almost 15,000 service user words, together with tables, charts and selected themes, are included in the following three chapters.

CHAPTER 10

Demographics and Themes

Our study consisted of 50 people, 20 men and 30 women. Demographic Tables and Figures are shown below (Tables 10.1–10.12 and Figures 10.1 and 10.2).

Table 10.1 Ethnic Origin			
English	44	Australian	1
Scottish	1	Pakistani	1
Irish	1	Spanish	1
German born Romany Gypsy	1		

Ages ranged between 18 and 74. The majority of interviewees, 86 per cent, were aged between 25 and 54.

Table 10.2 Age			
	Total	Male	Female
18–20	2	1	1
21–24	4	3	1
25–34	19	11	8
35–44	14	3	11
45–54	10	2	8
55–64	0	0	0
65–74	1	0	1
Over 75	0	0	0

Table 10.3 Percentage Comparison by Age and Gender		
	Male (%)	Female (%)
18–34	30%	20%
35–74	10%	40%

Eighty-six per cent were single, divorced or separated, and 66 per cent were living alone or sharing currently because they were in hospital. Eighty-eight per cent were on long-term sickness or other benefits. Just one was full-time employed.

Table 10.4 Marital status/living with			
Marital Status		Living with	
Single	28	Alone	23
Divorced/Separated	15	Others/Shared	15
Married or Living As	6	Partner	4
Widowed	1	Partner and Children	4
		Single Parent	4

Table 10.5 Housing and Employment			
Housing		Employment	
Rented House/Flat	23	'Sick'/Benefits	44
Hospital	10	Unemployed	2
Own House/Flat	9	Housewife	2
Supported Accommodation	4	Full-Time Employment	1
Homeless	2	Prison	1
Prison	1		
Residential Home	1		

Table 10.6 Percentage Comparison of Domestic and Employment Themes	
Single/Divorced/Separated	86
Living Alone/Sharing – Because Currently in Hospital	66
'Sick'/Claiming Benefits	88

Fifty-eight per cent had a diagnosis of Borderline Personality Disorder, for 28 per cent it was Dissocial, and for the remaining 14 per cent, in their terms, the Personality Disorder diagnosis was unspecified.

Table 10.7 Personality Disorder Diagnoses			
	Total	Female	Male
Borderline Personality Disorder	29	23	6
Dissocial Personality Disorder	14	3	11
Unspecified Personality Disorder	7	4	3

An analysis of additional psychiatric diagnoses showed that 78 per cent had a diagnosis of depression and 60 per cent of anxiety.

Table 10.8 Additional Diagnoses			
Depression	39	Brain Injury	2
Anxiety	30	Post Natal Depression	2
Eating Disorder	17	Multiple Personality Disorder	2
Manic Depression	11	Obsessive Compulsive Personality Disorder	1
Obsessive Compulsive Disorder	10	Histrionic Personality Disorder	1
Schizophrenia	7	Alcoholism	1
Post Traumatic Stress Disorder	6	Agoraphobia	1
Panic Disorder	2		

LIVERPOOL JOHN MOORES UNIVERSITY
LEARNING SERVICES

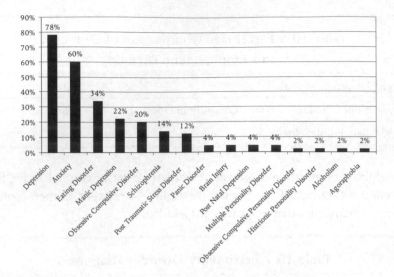

Figure 10.1 Percentage distribution of sample population with additional diagnosis

Eighty-six per cent of service users in this study described their difficulties in terms of depression or anxiety and often combinations of both. Morrison (1995) claims that the diagnosis of Personality Disorder is probably applied to a far greater proportion of patients than is necessary, because so many people can be shoehorned into its capacious definition. His consideration that many have more easily treatable disorders, including major depressive disorder, has importance for much of the sample for whom the diagnosis of depression had such relevance. Why had they been given, instead or in addition, a diagnosis of Personality Disorder, and were their difficulties more easily treatable? A psychiatric perspective may be that such a categorisation is merely that, a category which identifies a different type of disorder that is not mental illness, or is an associated disorder which may co-exist with mental illness, but is not a psychiatric illness. It exists, it needs to be recognised and categorised, but it is not our business because it is not a psychiatric illness. Inhabiting a hinterland devoid of real legitimacy this had left those so diagnosed disadvantaged from the start in terms of response and treatment.

Four interviewees had recently received a re-diagnosis of Bi-polar or Mood Disorder. All four did not consider they had experienced early abuse. This 8 per cent of respondents, who had managed to rid themselves of the diagnosis, were articulate and not slow to express their grievances. It may be that they had originally received a diagnosis of Personality Disorder because they were perceived as troublemakers. However, a question existed, was there a link among the remainder? The findings revealed that their exceptionalism was defined by early trauma and often brutal life experiences. Eighty-eight per cent had suffered abuse, violent, sexual and/or emotional, and for 80 per cent this was childhood abuse.

Table 10.9 Percentage of Abuse			
Total Abuse	88%	Childhood Abuse	80%

Symptomatology, outlined in Table 10.10, shows notably high rates of suicidality, 82 per cent, and self-harming behaviours, 88 per cent, confirming the extensive empirical support for the concept of a Post Traumatic Syndrome in survivors of prolonged and repeated victimisation (Herman and Van der Kolk 1987).

Table 10.10 Experiences					
Cutting	32	Destroying Things	28	Disassociated/ Separate	28
Other Types of Self-harm	24	Being Exploited	23	Imprisonment	19
Overdosing	39	Exploiting Others	3	Relationship Difficulties	41
Suicide Attempts	41	Hospitalisation	44	Abandonment	25
Alcohol Misuse	23	'Sectioned'	30	Loss of Children	19
Drug Abuse	15	Juvenile Convictions	6	Early Sexual Abuse	21
Overwhelming Anger	37	Adult Convictions	25	Early Violent Abuse	23
Desire to Hurt Others	24	Rejection from Services	25	Early Emotional Abuse	39
Violence to Others	21	Isolation	39	Later Abuse	30

A further analysis of Personality Disorder diagnoses showed a clear gender bias in that over 75 per cent of Borderline diagnoses were women, and over 75 per cent of Dissocial diagnoses were men (see Figure 10.2).

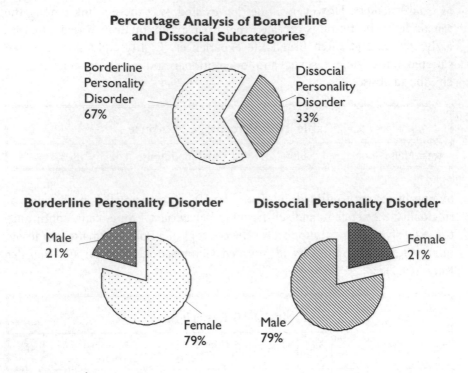

Figure 10.2 Gender Comparison

A comparison of selected themes showed that 20 per cent of the study were women who had been violent to others and 22 per cent were men. None of the men with a Borderline diagnosis had been violent to others. Thirty-five per cent of the women with a Borderline diagnosis had engaged in violent acts yet had retained the Borderline categorisation, suggesting the possibility that violence in men might attract a diagnosis of psychopathy more easily than in women (Prins 1995). Does this highlight the greater likelihood of a prison disposal on the basis of gender? Certainly, 26 per cent of the study were men who had experienced prison, compared to 12 per cent of women. Fifty per cent of the men with a Dissocial diagnosis considered their strengths to be care and compassion. Rather than the stereotypical notion of the psychopath viewing fellow human beings as 'empty vessels', they characterised themselves as 'Jekyll and Hyde', an embodiment of both compassion and aggression. They high-lighted the fact that aggression has a context, and that strengths may go unrecognised. This might best be illustrated by the respondent in our sample, in prison for an assault conviction, who had also received an 'Essex Man of the

Theme	Total (%)	Female (%)	Male (%)	Borderline Female (%)	Borderline Male (%)	Dissocial Female (%)	Dissocial Male (%)	Unspecified Female (%)	Unspecified Male (%)
Sample	100	60	40	46	12	6	22	6	8
Self-Harm	88	54	34	91	83	100	82	75	100
Suicidality	82	52	30	96	67	67	64	100	75
Violence to others	42	20	22	35	0	67	64	0	100
Imprisonment	38	12	26	13	50	67	73	33	50
Early Sexual Abuse	42	36	6	70	17	33	9	33	25
Early Violent Abuse	46	28	18	51	17	0	55	67	50
Early Emotional Abuse	78	50	28	87	50	100	73	67	75

Table 10.11 Percentage Analysis of Selected Themes

Year' award for saving a girl from a rape attack. Whether the categorisation is Borderline or Dissocial, our study shows high incidences of early abuse, self-harm and suicidality across categories. Women with a Dissocial diagnosis in our study all had a history of early emotional abuse, but none had a history of childhood violence, yet 67 per cent had been violent to others. Where men had experienced early violent abuse, some went on to harm others, some engaged in self-harm. These findings suggest that violence does not necessarily beget violence but that early, unresolved and unassimilated trauma can result in the perpetration of harm. This may be directed inwards as self-harm or outwards as harm to others. This questions the validity of the diagnosis of Personality Disorder and the subcategories within it.

Interviewees' comments on services and the professional attitudes they would like in an ideal world revealed a strong desire for a more humane response to Personality Disorder. In the following two chapters service users comment fully and directly regarding what has helped them most, including the types of therapeutic interventions that are available and helpful. Specific support systems are rated in Table 10.12.

Table 10.12 Percentage Comparison of Support

	% Responding	Very Helpful (%)	Helpful (%)	OK (%)	Not Helpful (%)	Harmful (%)	Helpful/Harmful Split (%)
Family	100	10	16	8	24	22	20
Friends	100	22	32	28	16	2	0
Church and Spiritual Beliefs	64	34	22	13	22	9	0
Hospital	92	2	30	33	26	7	2
Day Hospital	70	0	23	37	31	6	3
Therapeutic Community	22	27	10	18	18	27	0
Safe House/Crisis House	4	50	0	50	0	0	0
Voluntary Centres	64	56	22	16	6	0	0
Colchester MHT	86	12	23	18	33	12	2
Colchester Joint MHT	42	14	24	24	29	9	0
Police	70	9	11	26	17	34	3
Solicitor	78	38	29	18	10	5	0
Armed Forces	12	17	17	0	0	66	0
Supported Housing	32	25	31	0	31	13	0
Medication	100	18	28	26	18	8	2
Psychiatrist	96	13	15	19	20	23	10
Psychotherapist/ Counsellor	86	25	30	15	25	5	0
Nurse	80	12	33	35	10	8	2
Occupational Therapist	54	22	19	33	22	4	0
Mental Health Social Worker	50	28	16	24	24	8	0
Child Protection Social Worker	30	0	13	0	20	67	0
Advocate	90	71	27	2	0	0	0
Accident and Emergency	86	20	16	32	30	2	0
General Hospital	86	26	26	26	18	4	0
GP	100	36	24	18	16	6	0

'Family' was included in the highest category of a helpful/harmful split of 20 per cent. Respondents ticked very helpful and harmful or, for example, wrote 'mother' against helpful and 'father' against harmful. The only other high rating for helpful/harmful split was psychiatrists, at 10 per cent. Here again both helpful and harmful boxes were ticked, indicating a possibility that psychiatrists, who are sometimes seen to head the professional hierarchy, might be perceived by service users as good or bad parental/authority figure. Where appreciation was expressed about psychiatrists, a democratic approach is suggested. 'He has treated me as an intellectual equal and doesn't talk down to me.'

Many disciplines, from primary and secondary care, included positive or fair responses. GPs rated well at 60 per cent helpful or very helpful. Voluntary centres, for those who had attended them, received a very good rating of 78 per cent very helpful or helpful, and none harmful. Thirty-two per cent of respondents indicated that they had experienced supported housing. This appears to have received a mixed response, although more helpful than harmful. Only two respondents had encountered a crisis or safe house. For one it was very helpful, for the other just OK. Twenty-two per cent of the sample had experiences of Therapeutic Communities. The rating here is unexpectedly low. On closer examination, only two respondents attended communities dedicated to the treatment of self-harm or Personality Disorder. For one, it was the most helpful and positive of experiences. For the other, the service user concerned considered that the timing was wrong. 'I think it was too soon for this therapy. I wasn't ready.' Remaining communities were mainly residential drug and alcohol rehabilitation facilities. Medication was given a fair-to-mixed response. Hospitals and community mental health teams did not rate high as helpful, reinforcing one view that traumatised people are vulnerable to becoming revictimised and may engage in 'destructive' interactions with mental health services which they tend to relate to as they would to parents, enacting early abusive developmental roles (Dunn and Parry 1997). The police and child protection social workers scored high as unhelpful and harmful, saying something regarding the coercive nature of such agencies and, again, about revictimisation. Advocates and solicitors scored high as helpful or very helpful, suggesting the need for someone who is 'on my side'.

Psychotherapeutic interventions and counselling rated well as helpful and are commented on further and most favourably by service users in the following two chapters. Two main features here are Cognitive Analytic Therapy (CAT) and interventions from occupational therapists. OTs in North Essex often employ a cognitive and solution focused approach and sometimes use Penny Parks' (1990) Inner Child Therapy. 'There was a lot of writing letters, making things real and having to sign them, and visualisations. I found it difficult, but I was happy with this therapy.'

The section of our findings headed 'The Therapy Experience' in Chapter 12 throws particular light on what has been helpful and what not. What appears to have been unhelpful is group psychotherapy. 'I spent eighteen months saying nothing' and 'I had psychotherapy. It was terrible. I didn't understand it at all. It was group psychotherapy. I did it for a year and said nothing.' In our study, during the course of the interview respondents may have referred to experiences of early abuse but very few elaborated on the details. Some did not mention abuse at all during the interview schedule but ticked boxes indicating that such abuse had, in fact, occurred. One conclusion here is that, although it may be possible to refer to such experiences in a surface way, a deeper exploration can be very difficult, especially within a group. 'I wasn't prepared to talk about what had gone on in my early life.' For some, the dynamic interaction and fruitful learning which group psychotherapy can provide may not be something they were able to benefit from at this time.

Roth and Fonagy (1997), in their analysis *What Works for Whom?*, concluded that Psychodynamic Psychotherapy had limited effectiveness, while Dialectical Behaviour Therapy (DBT) was the most effective treatment for Personality Disorder. Individual psychotherapy is not something which has emerged here as a helpful intervention. Cognitive Behavioural Therapy (CBT) had helped some for a limited time. It may be that those with this diagnosis appreciate a more functional and interactive approach where the emphasis is not all on the client to bring something to the discussion. Ego strength may be poor amongst this client group, and their self-esteem low. Emphasis in a cognitive approach is on partnership, which might be perceived as more 'holding'. This also has relevance for some mothers in our study, who found the 'Pandora's box' of a therapeutic experience to have too frightening and profound an effect on their feelings. Disabling at times, this affected their ability to function as parents, meaning loss of their children. Support and coping skills may have proved more effective in such situations.

Twelve per cent of respondents considered Cognitive Analytic Therapy (CAT) to have been the type of therapy that helped most. 'He's done more than the whole services put together.' A consideration of the kind of dissociative states experienced by some in this client group, described in Chapter 12, helps to give an appreciation of the kind of distorted sense of self which is experienced. Self states had resulted in suicide attempts of such lethality that survival seemed miraculous. One respondent threw herself down a sheer forty-foot cliff face and survived. Anger had become dammed up behind a narrow response function. Etched in red against the background of a beautiful young arm was the word 'hate'. Where early life had been sexually or violently abusive, or simply included an unloving and devastating non-response from care givers, the blunt limitations of their experience had left some stripped of control and disempowered beyond comprehension. Ryle's (1997) concept of CAT incorporates an integrative approach which fully acknowledges role limitation and the deeply powerful transference issues likely to arise. However, CAT is time limited.

> It's for twenty-four weeks. I've just started going deep into my past. As I've only got four weeks left, and my therapist has told me she's leaving, I now have to be brought up to coping level, which I think is very unfair because it's the first time I've told anyone about the abuse.

Ryle might be likely to respond to this dilemma by indicating that endings are, in themselves, part of the therapeutic process. Necessarily addressed at stages throughout therapy, they are seen to have a risk pattern adjustment function and are used to precipitate the retention of learning regarding loss. Perhaps the power of 'endings' should not be pre-judged before they have occurred. However, considering the degree of deprivation experienced by some clients, one might question whether 24 weeks is sufficient time to assimilate such trauma and dissociated parts of the personality. One respondent described the necessity of hospitalisation, at times of relapse, as new areas of trauma are approached in CAT therapy. CAT psychologists in this area appeared to be adopting a more flexible, open-ended, approach to such cases. 'I've seen him for over a year' and 'In some cases, like my own, it can continue without limit of time.' Dialectical Behaviour Therapy was not available in North Essex during the time of our research, however, we were to discover that DBT also contracts for at least one year (Kiehn and Swales 1995).

Where respondents in the study were receiving understanding, and more effective treatment, they usually had a Borderline diagnosis. The 'gurus' of Personality Disorder treatment invariably focus on psychological intervention for Borderline Personality Disorder (Bateman 1997; Fonagy 1997; Linehan 1999; Ryle 1997). Yet similar unassimilated trauma, and dissociated aspects of the personality, were also being experienced by those in our sample with a Dissocial diagnosis, suggesting that treatment strategies developed for those with a Borderline diagnosis may also have relevance for those diagnosed as Dissocial. 'I would like to see more credence given to people with Personality

Disorder, more research. I definitely don't want to be locked up as is currently being debated.'

The Henderson Hospital characterises itself as a centre devoted to the treatment of Personality Disorders per se. Only one respondent from our sample had attended the Henderson. Although diagnosed as Borderline, with a high degree of suicidality, adult convictions had also begun to accrue. A criminal justice disposal may have been a not unlikely future for this client. Although not claiming a complete 'cure', the progress made by this respondent supports the claim to effective treatment outcomes made by the Henderson Hospital (Dolan, Norton and Warren 1996). 'The most important thing was to be able to be in touch with my feelings and own my feelings – it allowed me to be empowered and be responsible for my own actions.'

High numbers responding to the rating categories for statutory support suggests that over the years our sample had been involved with a variety of mental health services. Eighty-eight per cent claimed to have experienced hospitalisation and 60 per cent had at some time been sectioned under the Mental Health Act. For a number, the association spanned decades; for others it was more than ten years. But are the kinds of support they had received likely to alleviate or sometimes to exacerbate difficulties? Many of the sample lived alone and experienced isolation; 88 per cent were 'sick' and receiving welfare benefits. Many were still depressed and anxious. The most often reported, and unpopular, professional response in our study was to be told one is 'attention seeking'. 'Told I was attention seeking – worst thing I could have been told because I was crying out for somebody to help me.' To say someone is attention seeking is to imply that person is not worthy of attention. It is dismissive. Professionals might rather see behaviours such as self-harm, continual neediness and suicide attempts as attachment seeking which might be better understood in terms of attachment theory and separation anxiety (Bowlby 1988).

Issues concerning knowledge, understanding, deservability and resource constraints may all have contributed to the colouring of response to this client group. However, in a client group which has a suicide expectancy of 15 per cent (DoH 1998), the question is whether the need for effective treatment strategies can be ignored. First, in human terms:

> I do so want to just curl up and die, to end this relentless misery once and for all. This existence is really terrible.

> I want to kill – think about killing all the time. If I was to kill it would make Hungerford look like a teddy bears' picnic.

And, second, in terms of ultimate cost-effectiveness:

> The local hospital won't take me – they hope and pray I will go away. But I
> will keep coming back and back until I am in my grave.

> Nobody is sure what CAT is going to get me in the end. I have changed
> over the past two years. I understand more. If there was more funding and
> more people with experience, I believe there could be an answer to all this.
> What I want is one whole personality – that's me.

> In an ideal world I would not need any of the services.

In the following two chapters service users in the study report further, and com-
prehensively, on questions regarding their condition, experiences, diagnoses
and treatment.

CHAPTER 11

What Personality Disorder Means to Us

The following quotes from service users were given as a response to the questionnaire featured in Chapter 8 (Figure 8.1).

1. WHAT DOES PERSONALITY DISORDER MEAN TO YOU?

13 people = Don't know – 26% of total questioned

Haven't been told what it means.

Haven't got a clue.

It means nothing to me.

11 = A label you get when 'they' don't know what else to do – 22%

I've been given the label because they don't know what to make of me.

Being rubbished by clinical staff.

When it's not easy to diagnose what you've got, you're given the label.

A label they put on people when they can't treat or figure out what's wrong with you.

An utter load of baloney.

LIVERPOOL
JOHN MOORES UNIVERSITY
AVRIL ROBARTS LRC
TITHEBARN STREET
LIVERPOOL L2 2ER
TEL: 0151 231 4022

It means the services don't know what to do with you.

A dustbin label given to people who seem difficult.

A term psychiatrists use when they can't come up with a diagnosis.

9 = Mood swings/Personality change – 18%

Jekyll and Hyde.

Becoming a different person.

Can't control my temper – use drink and drugs to blot things out.

Jekyll and Hyde – become totally different.

Personality swings without knowing about it.

Brain acts differently to other people – could swing out of control at any time.

Flipping from one emotion to another.

Being like Jekyll and Hyde.

5 = Bad/Labelled – 10%

Bad and evil – born with your personality.

It means you're a psychopath.

Life sentence – untreatable – no hope.

Being classified as abnormal.

3 = Identity – 6%

I don't know who I am.

No personality.

Don't know who I am.

3 = Developmental – 6%

A problem in how the personality has developed which doesn't come under the specification for mental illness.

I didn't develop emotionally as a child.

It's where you're affected in early life – like a computer with some data missing.

3 = Self-destructive – 6%

Harmful and destructive to self.

Self-destructive, and sometimes towards others – extreme difficulty with life, relationships and communicating.

2 = Relationship difficulties – 4%

Problems with relationships.

Difficulties in relating to people.

1 = Dissociation – 2%

My mind and body are separate. I'm angry and disappointed and not able to cope.

2. HOW DID YOU FIND OUT ABOUT YOUR PERSONALITY DISORDER DIAGNOSIS?

28 = Psychiatrists – 56%

I asked at review – the psychiatrist told me very reluctantly.

He told me I had Personality Disorder. I asked what kind? He said unspecified. He went on to describe Personality Disorder in a very critical way. This left me feeling insulted.

In 1980 a psychiatrist told my mother and she told me. I didn't know for a long time.

I asked the consultant.

During a remand assessment in prison.

In Chelmsford prison when the psychiatrist visited to do a pre-court assessment. The fucking bitch got me six months for breaking a window.

I was first diagnosed at 16. It made me feel abnormal.

Only one doctor told me. All the others before that said I had manic depression.

I asked the consultant what my diagnosis was… I felt insulted, angry and I felt I was given a label that implied it was my fault.

I had a meeting with 25 doctors. The outcome was that they considered I had Personality Disorder, but my own consultant told me afterwards that he didn't like to label people.

When the doctor talked to me about my feelings, he's the only one that got it anywhere near right.

The psychiatrist told me after I asked.

It came from a psychiatrist when I was told I had no feelings.

A psychiatrist told me about twenty years ago. My reaction was that they must think I'm daft.

The doctor told me in hospital. It made me depressed, angry and anxious.

A psychiatrist changed my diagnosis in 1998 – for four years previously I had been diagnosed with bi-polar disorder.

At the review nobody took time to explain the diagnosis to me and all the discussions took place about me, but not involving me. I remember feeling numb and bewildered, as if everyone knew except me. I felt as if there was little or no hope for me.

Basically, a group of doctors told me I had Personality Disorder…don't give a fuck.

It was an insult because somebody didn't like my personality.

After seven years in the services I found out from a psychiatrist. I asked how the diagnosis was made. He didn't give me an answer.

The psychiatrist said I'd got Personality Disorder. I wondered what it meant.

8 = Reports and records – 16%

I found out from a tribunal report. I can't remember the psychiatrist ever having talked to me directly about it.

After I was discharged I opened a letter from my psychiatrist to the GP – it said it there. I was a bit stumped – shocked. I'd heard about people that had been diagnosed with Personality Disorder being the black sheep of the community. It made me feel I didn't belong anywhere.

I asked for access to my notes and found out about Personality Disorder.

I'd been through a lot to make me feel bad about myself, but felt I could overcome it. I found out from the psychiatrist's report for a child care case. It was the first time I knew. It made me feel very low about myself – helpless.

I read my notes upside down by accident. I have never been told officially.

I've not been told by a doctor – it was implied in a social worker's report for a child protection meeting.

When I asked to view my records it was in a letter to my GP from a psychiatrist. I was concerned about others reading it and if it would cloud how I would be treated. Four other psychiatrists have all given me a diagnosis of depression.

I received a copy of the tribunal report. I was surprised. It took a while to come to terms with it. That was the first I'd heard of it.

4 = Inferred – 8%

I've been given no diagnosis – but I fit the bill.

I was never told, I guessed.

I believed that I had Personality Disorder without anyone telling me – it was confirmed at the Henderson.

3 = Advocate – 6%

I gave her permission to ask. I thought – what are they on about?

I found out from my advocate, who found out from [a professional].

My advocate found out at a meeting I refused to attend. Nobody has told me. My feelings are nothing.

3 = Social worker – 6%

My social worker told me for my DLA (Disability Living Allowance) form. It made me think that part of my personality is not right.

I felt very depressed by the diagnosis.

Social Services suddenly mentioned it at a child protection conference. I was shocked and gobsmacked and couldn't believe it.

2 = GP – 4%

I was told by my GP.

Told by three GPs – It means nothing to me personally, I have two degrees and nine '0' levels.

2 = Nurse – 4%

I asked a nurse. I thought – I've got to get out of this. Then I felt numb to anything anybody said.

I asked my co-worker and she found it in my notes. I thought – that's it – I don't stand a chance of getting any help.

3. IF YOU WERE GIVEN A FREE HAND TO DESCRIBE WHAT YOU CONSIDER TO BE YOUR PROBLEMS, WHAT WOULD YOU SAY?

18 = Depression/Depression plus other – 36%

I get depressed – thoughts of self-harm and harming others – the voices are terrifying – at times there's no control – desperate – a loner.

Mostly chronic depression – hear voices – self-harm – anorexia.

Depression – tired all the time.

Very depressed – useless – worthless – no self-esteem or confidence – no hope – I have been crushed by the past.

Depression – low self-esteem – self-harm – anxiety – vulnerable – lonely – inability to express anger appropriately – no confidence.

Depression – paranoid.

Depression may lift with pills or talking treatments, but there's nothing for Personality Disorder – I self-harm.

Depression and schizophrenia.

I am manic depressive which requires a careful balance of medication – notably a mood stabiliser.

Depression and anxiety – eating disorder.

Really bad depression with voices and sometimes psychosis – they said I didn't have a psychotic episode when I was screaming at voices.

Either too high or too low – I've heard voices and experienced visual hallucinations and I have a bad temper. I have tried to kill myself – cut and taken overdoses. I've also tried to set light to my head.

Depression – anxiety – difficult relationships – feeling cut off from the world – an outsider sleeping problems – sexual problems.

Depression.

Depression – hear voices – used to harm myself.

Very up and down – moods aggressive – hard to trust people – since the diagnosis I've turned to drink.

Depression – my mind doesn't work properly – I feel anxious all the time.

14 = Abuse/Blaming self – 28%

Suffering the effects of being sexually abused as a child – depression – panic – bulimia – don't belong – anxiety – stress – insomnia – self-harm.

Violent first marriage.

Nightmares filled with guilt about people you had to kill in the line of duty – and they can't understand the living nightmare – I don't like crowds and closed-in spaces.

The reason is I was brought up as a girl and not a boy.

Things that have gone on in my life since being a little girl – it's also drugs related.

I've had many traumas since these men fucked me up the bum. I blame myself. I just feel abnormal.

Feel I'm to blame – need to cut to release blame – can't make a marriage work – husband is kept in hospital – if he came out I would kill him.

My problems really start from a young age when I lost my mother due to a heroin overdose.

I was born to live with a bastard of a so-called father who used me as a punch bag and hit the shit out of me.

I couldn't forgive myself for past events in my life – self-harm regularly by cutting or taking tablets – low self-esteem – no confidence.

Irreparable damage called treatment.

A violent marriage and post natal depression.

A bad childhood – living in fear comes from the childhood – panic attacks, sexual problems, alcohol and drug addiction – fear of coping alone – depression.

11 = Stress/Not coping – 22%

Dealing with stresses and changes in life – cutting – self-harming – overdosing.

Extreme stress – anxiety, depression, paranoia – feeling of isolation.

Homeless – no money – no one gives a toss.

Couldn't cope – post natal depression – couldn't talk about things in the past.

Lack of security – lack of help – need people around me – hormone problems.

I have a large problem in dealing with compound stress.

Feel unable to cope with the stresses of life – let people wind me up – anxiety – bottled-up feelings – fear of rejection – problems stem from childhood.

Very big sense of not being able to cope – I cut myself because I can't cope and that makes me feel better. Hear voices, see things that aren't there.

I'm confused – can't get a job because of my prison record – my mum doesn't want to help me – I damage things – have lost my temper with guns and knives – told I can't be helped.

When I get stressed I forget things like the day and date and things people say – feel I'm tied in a knot and trying to untangle myself – causes acid indigestion which makes me sick – I binge and have comfort food which reassures me at the time.

7 = Substance misuse – 14%

Heavy drugs – LSD and heroin.

Alcohol and drug abuse, paracetamol, medication, laxatives – depression, anxiety and eating disorder.

Used to drink a lot before I took medication. I have an attitude problem that changes me into someone else.

Alcohol – suffer with depression and have taken overdoses at times of stress.

Alcohol – I like a good piss-up.

Addiction – low self-esteem.

Heavy drugs – heroin – parents splitting up – I have never seen two people hate each other as much as they did in the end.

4. WOULD YOU PLEASE TELL ME WHAT YOU THINK YOUR STRENGTHS ARE?

19 = Caring – 38%

I care a lot about people.

I think I have strong compassion – I'm a good listener.

I have a caring attitude and enjoy helping others. I was also made Man of the Year in Essex for saving a girl from a rape attack.

I've been told that when I'm well I'm a lovely person – caring.

Listening to people – caring for them.

Deep down I am a caring person. I try to help people in my own way.

My strength is that I'm good with kids. I would never, never hurt them, only the people who hurt children – I'll kill them with my bare hands.

I try to listen to other people and give them a chance. I do voluntary work – sometimes this can affect me, sometimes it makes me feel better.

I try to be kind to other people and animals – intelligent, well-educated, honest, good at art and writing.

Good mum – kind and caring   put the kids first – produce plenty of milk – a good cow.

Being able to talk about problems and get on with people – cooking, rug making and floristry.

People say I'm caring – dressmaking and cake making – these I do when I'm well.

Caring – a fighter – good at being a nurse.

Being patient with people – being nice.

14 = Endurance/Strength – 28%

Strength to survive – because of my daughter – I help run a mother and toddler group.

Will-power – to fight the drugs and get my kids back.

Stubbornness – if I wasn't I wouldn't be here today.

I'm a strong person – determined.

I'm a strong person – I've got a lot to give.

Determined to get better, artistic and willing to change.

I'm very strong willed and stubborn.

Capability to cope with whatever happens.

Flexibility – good with animals

A lot of determination.

Knowing I've got a choice of living or dying.

Tenacity.

I have a strong ability to adapt.

6 = Have none – 12%

I don't think I have any.

I have no strengths, just a mass of weaknesses.

4 = Creative – 8%

The only thing I've ever been good at is art – I can draw but I can't read and write.

Cooking, sewing and knitting.

Creative, generous, neat and tidy.

Computers, art and cookery.

4 = Religious beliefs – 8%

Faith in religion – pottery and keep-fit.

Jesus is the strength I don't have.

I am a committed Christian.

Religion has helped my tormented soul to come to terms with what has happened.

1 = Humour – 2%

A sense of humour – loyal and reliable – good at my job when I worked.

1 = Expressiveness – 2%

I'm more direct now about my feelings – less weighed down with issues of the past – I put this down to my stay at the Henderson.

1 = Intelligent – 2%

Very psychologically active and quite accidentally clever.

5. COULD YOU PLEASE TALK ABOUT ANY IMPLICATIONS YOU THINK THE DIAGNOSIS HAD FOR HOW YOU HAVE BEEN SUPPORTED/TREATED?

22 = Treated badly – 44%

Staff didn't want to know.

I became a 'services leper' – told by the psychiatrist I had been blacklisted. After the diagnosis was made I felt excluded – general unwillingness to help – refused treatment.

Consultant told me there was nothing wrong with me and I didn't need medication – I banged my fists against the wall and he threatened to call the police.

It's 'hands off – give her a wide berth'. My own GP throws his arms in the air – has actually said he doesn't know what to do with me – feels like he's given up.

Treated less sympathetically because of Personality Disorder – not mental illness – something you've brought on yourself.

Treated rough and kept in hospital for three-and-a-half years – out on Home Office licence – mustn't put a foot wrong or I'm back in.

Told I was attention seeking – worst thing I could have been told because I was crying out for somebody to help – I've been treated like shit.

It took a long time to get into hospital. The A & E doctor called the duty psychiatrist – when he knew who I was I was told to go home without seeing anyone – thought I was doing the responsible thing to do something before things got bad – I had self-harmed.

A lot of people see you as untreatable – you're not offered the help and support. You're not seen as a human being but as a diagnosis – everything you do is seen in that light.

Treatment is pretty poor – there are not enough options available – people seem to be scared of the diagnosis.

The local hospital won't take me – they hope and pray I go away. But I will keep coming back and back until I am in my grave.

I can't have therapy until I've stopped self-harming, but I can't stop self-harming until I've had therapy – they don't care about what you think is wrong with you, they only listen to the bits you say that fit in with their diagnosis.

With panic disorder and depression I received help – with Personality Disorder I was treated differently – I had no help.

I was made to wait while others were seen straight away. The doctor never lifted his head when I was in the room, he carried on as if I wasn't there.

I've been treated very unfairly – so rudely – without respect – like an idiot. It's either secure hospital or no support at all.

Once they decided I wasn't schizophrenic the services just dumped me. They don't talk about the real problems – I feel they've given up on me.

I have been treated like an idiot – as if what I thought and was feeling didn't matter.

I think the diagnosis is saying 'troublemaker'. You're ignored – people can be hostile – you're not taken seriously. People don't believe there's anything wrong with you if you've got Personality Disorder.

10 = Mixed/Improved – 20%

There's two groups of people, those who try to understand and those who think you're just attention seeking and you don't deserve treatment.

It was a long time before I was properly treated. Lived everywhere – I was in the night shelter – picked up by the police in a nunnery – got medication sorted in hospital and good accommodation – been well for four years.

Just lately I get treated like a human being.

Some people helped – I was lucky some nurses rise above their job description.

I wasn't treated in the past because they didn't think they could help me. I ended up in a top security hospital. I'm currently diagnosed as mentally ill and Personality Disordered, but the mental illness went unrecognised for approximately six years.

Staff's conduct left a lot to be desired – a minority did not credit me with any feelings and were dismissive and unsupportive because of the Personality Disorder label – others were excellent.

Before I went to the Henderson I was treated with contempt. People didn't understand why I was behaving the way I was.

I get better treatment now – a special counsellor – the right medication – I get responses more quickly from my GP and CPN.

In one area they may give you help, in another area you don't get help. It's very patchy.

5 = No difference – 10%

No way I was treated any different.

I see no difference to how anybody else would be treated.

Has made no difference whatsoever.

It made no difference, I was treated the same as everybody else.

4 = Treated badly by Social Services – 8%

Unfairly treated – losing my children and not giving me support to get them back.

I have had a rough time with Social Services. They took my kids away last week. How do you tell a four-year-old and a ten-year-old they are being taken away?

I've been treated like I'm a mad parent, instead of an ill parent or disabled person. I'm treated like I'm not trying hard enough.

2 = Good support – 4%

I've had a lot of good support through the social worker and psychiatrist together.

I've been treated pretty well.

2 = Picked up by police – 4%

Major problem with the police – arrested for being drunk and disorderly.

The police gave me hassle and tried to beat me up. When they knew I was ex-military they changed and treated me with more respect.

2 = Not sure – 4%

I don't know if it's made a difference or not.

Don't really know – just found out since April.

2 = Caused by self – 4%

I've allowed myself to be treated really badly in life.

I have always turned my back on support and treatment and have been anti everything.

1 = Treated differently in prison – 2%

In prison was treated different – door was unlocked – I was given a needle up the bum once a week.

RESPONSES TO QUESTION SIX ARE INCLUDED IN CHAPTER 12.

7. WHAT WOULD YOU LIKE IN AN IDEAL WORLD, OR WHAT WOULD YOU REALLY LIKE TO SEE HAPPEN TO YOU AND THE SERVICES YOU ARE INVOLVED WITH?

17 = Better service response – 34%

To be listened to, treated with respect, understood – people who are straight-up and honest and will help you.

To be listened to and respected and not to have my pain ignored and unheld.

They should take time out to explain in more detail about illness, instead of giving you loads of drugs – not to have mixed wards.

Less medication, more talking to find deep-rooted problems. Not to give the diagnosis willy-nilly when there's so much stigma attached.

Standard of treatment in the private sector to be available to everyone – services need to come under scrutiny.

System should be changed – challenged legally – bungalow – girlfriend – a hand with the shopping.

I would like more one-to-one.

For staff to listen and take things seriously – chance for an in-depth consultation – feel secure – safety net.

No continuity of care – people fixate on self-harm. They need to look at why people self-harm – need to be looked at as a whole person, not just a collection of symptoms. I could start psychotherapy.

More collaboration amongst services – more interaction with the person on what their needs are and not what professionals think the needs are.

Treat me like a human being and not an animal – I am a human being with feelings and I want to be treated just like everybody else.

More co ordination   keeping an eye on who they employ.

Staff to change their attitude and become more sympathetic – spend more time with me.

The system to understand me, like listening – me to talk more – afraid to talk.

To keep trying me on different drugs to get rid of the voices – for the doctor to stop laughing at me – the Services to be blown up by the IRA – a special clinic for Personality Disorder.

More understanding and not just fill me up with pills and send me on my way and for them to communicate with each other.

6 = Out of hours/Safe house/Helpline – 12%

Safe house – some organisation to get in touch with out of hours.

Crisis house, crisis team, more out-of-hours support – somewhere to go when you're feeling desperate.

A 24-hour hot-line. If I had problems I could phone – they'd tap in a PIN in the computer for my file – to be accepted – only one personality is accepted – the adult.

I think a half-way house would be a good idea – people understanding about the diagnosis – better forms of treatment.

Safe house – no one turned away – 24-hour phone line – someone to talk to – pull forces together in same direction – one guideline for everybody so nobody gets confused.

6 = Label changed or responded to differently – 12%

Terminology rephrased and brought up to date – more personalised programme for individuals – more public awareness, and a better understanding from GPs upwards.

It should be more clearly defined and there should be substantial evidence to make a diagnosis over a lengthy time of assessment.

There should be no such thing as Personality Disorder.

Get rid of the Personality Disorder label – care in the community to improve, and I mean in a big way

I would like to see more credence given to people with Personality Disorder – more research – I definitely don't want to be locked up as currently being debated.

5 = Activities/Occupation – 10%

I need more activities to do.

To work part or full time.

More activity towards work training – a lot more safe and secure housing.

Better facilities – more activities – more stimulation.

4 = Home and family – 8%

A wife, family, better nurses - have a meal in a restaurant.

To be living in my own place with support from all the services I'm in contact with.

Reunited with my husband.

House, wife, kids – all that crap.

4 = Better parenting help – 8%

When my child was a baby, to help me bond – specialist centre for parents with mental health problems – some acknowledgement from anybody that I have got a problem.

Off drugs long term – losing my kids brought it home to me – you don't know how lucky you are until you lose it.

For Social Services to go away and let me lead a normal life.

To still have my daughter. I'd like to be a family.

3 = Don't know – 6%

I don't know any more – I'm terrified in case another man tries it on with me.

I don't think I can stay in the world. I don't want anything.

2 = Safe world for children – 4%

All kids in my world would never be hurt – let me get my hands on the bastards. I'll teach them what it's like to rape and strangle. I'll kill them first...you get my drift?

Above all, a non-threatening world to bring up children, a world where *no* meant *no*.

1 = Not to need services – 2%

In an ideal world I would not need any of the services.

1 = Less urban alienation – 2%

There are two paths...you walk into the first garden and there are animals, trees, fruit and vegetables, friends and rivers...and in the second garden you find concrete, pollution, industrial chemical waste, no animals, heroin, crack and all sorts of pills – this sums up how I feel... I would chose the first garden in my ideal world.

1 = Second chance – 2%

To be given another chance in life, that's all I ask.

WHAT WOULD YOU SAY ARE THE THINGS WHICH HAVE HELPED YOU MOST?

(More than one answer given by most respondents.)

18 – Family – 36%

Mum

Parents

Brother

Girlfriend

Brother

Father-in-law

Mum and Dad

Girlfriend

Mum

Partner – supportive – sticks by me.

Mother very supportive.

Ex-wife has managed to take a lot – police – courts – and also knows why.

My daughter – she's challenged me and diverted my thoughts.

Partner has had to put up with a lot – believes in me – supports and encourages me.

Mum – she's the best in the world – if it wasn't for my mum and sister I wouldn't be here today.

Mum – she puts up with a lot – where would I be without her?

17 = Therapists – 34%

CAT therapy

Occupational Therapist

Psychologist – CAT

Psychologist – CAT

CAT therapist

My counsellor – she has given me a lot of support and has gone beyond what they do.

Counsellor – new on the scene – feel I can work with her – we click – finding it very helpful.

Psychologist – CAT – I've seen him for over a year. He's done more than the whole services put together.

Care co-ordinator/OT – psychological help – been there for me – given me support and counselling – been what I've needed over the last couple of years.

Occupational Therapist – easy to talk to – honest and straightforward – writes notes with me so I know exactly what went into them – constructive suggestions.

Occupational Therapist – is down to earth – supportive – makes time for me.

OT – a good listener.

Therapist – she will help me and not leave me.

Henderson Hospital – don't think I would have passed 30 due to the way I was behaving.

Psychologist – CAT – it's taken me a while – I can talk about anything – he is also very understanding.

Private psychologist – he talked to me and that helped. He had time and wasn't rushed. He got me back driving – cost me a £100 a session and I had to give it up.

17 = Advocacy – 34%

Advocacy has been there for me.

My advocate's been marvellous.

Sorts things out

Supports and understands.

Has been more than helpful.

A good listener.

Was always there when I wanted her.

Advocacy's brill.

Has done a lot – negotiated leave, helped with medication and child care issues – recommended solicitors – loads of letters.

Helps with debts and threatened court cases. She helps with the practical stuff.

Knew who to go to when I wasn't feeling well – went to my reviews with me.

Gone to meetings for me – very supportive.

Impartial – objective in a good way.

13 = Medication – 26%

Modern medicine was best – no side effects.

Medication helped calm me down and give me a jolt back to reality.

Helps me feel better.

Made me feel better although it took a long time to kick in.

By helping stabilise my mood.

Helps my moods.

Tranquillisers – anti-depressants ease the depression.

Makes me feel happier.

Has calmed me down – also able to get out and about.

To calm me down and keep my thoughts in order.

Helps numb the pain, but not deal with it.

12 = Voluntary sector – 24%

Open Road

Mind Centre

Colchester Mind

Mind Day Centre

AA

Mind Centre

Mind Centre – Halstead

Open Road

Chelmsford Mind

Eating Disorders Centre – safe there.

Eating Disorders – somebody to talk to and not feel lonely.

Social worker – Oxford Road.

Self-help groups – 'Defeat Depression'.

National Schizophrenia Fellowship – they've been brilliant.

Open Road – a chat and coffee – somewhere to go.

12 = Psychiatrists/Hospital/Hospital keyworker – 24%

Psychiatrist – she was very kind and helpful.

Consultant in Colchester, not Clacton, she made things safer for me during pregnancy.

Psychiatrist in hospital.

Psychiatrist – he has treated me as an intellectual equal and doesn't talk down to me.

Going to rehab ward and getting medication sorted.

Hospital stopped me harming myself.

Royal Edinburgh – good brain injury unit.

Hospitals – they've made me a man – cared for me.

Good keyworker – saw her regularly in hospital and got on well.

Keyworker – Willow House.

Keyworker continuity and not having to explain yourself day in and day out.

11 = Community Mental Health Teams – 22%

Social worker

CPN

NEEDAS [North East Essex Drug and Alcohol Service]

Good CPN – sat and listened – came regularly.

Good social worker – came regularly and advised me on what to do.

Support worker – comes once a week and takes me out.

Social worker – regular contact when in a crisis – but this is a recent thing.

Keyworker in the community comes and sees me every two weeks – listens and supports.

CPN – weekly visits from one – no other CPNs were helpful.

CPN puts my mind at rest.

Social worker – beings me back to reality – puts things in perspective, and support worker helped get me back into the community – got me a place at college and some voluntary work.

7 = GPs – 14%

Excellent – good listener.

New GP – quick treatment.

GP helped most.

Present GP has helped me medically and spiritually.

A very nice man – he cares for me.

7 = Friends – 14%

Being there and being supportive.

Friends have been very supportive.

Encouragement and support from good friends – being loved.

Friend listens to me – takes strolls with me – through her I can go anywhere.

5 = Other clients – 10%

Similar experiences.

Talking to others with the same or similar problems.

Understanding – we get on really well.

Being with people at North Gate Day Centre and Work-on.

5 = Church/Spiritual beliefs – 10%

Spiritual support

Church and spiritual beliefs

Faith

Faith in the Lord Jesus Christ.

4 = Accommodation – 8%

Residential home.

The right kind of supported accommodation – not with old men.

Supported housing – there if you need them – genuine, nice people.

Had some problems with neighbours – but now I've been moved into suitable accommodation – I feel safer.

2 = Child Care – 4%

Home Start helped with the kids – taking them out – general support.

Foster and day care   helped me to be able to look after my own needs.

2 = Education – 4%

Educational background.

College boosted confidence – challenging – energising – given me a purpose – treated more like a human being.

2 = Independence/Individuation – 4%

Being left alone to live my own life.

Ignoring the outside world.

2 = Creativity – 4%

Writing, music and being able to express myself.

Music.

2 = Self-harm – 4%

Self-harm – it's like a release.

Self-harm helps as this is a way of coping. If I didn't self-harm I'd be more suicidal.

2 = Solicitors – 4%

1 = Incontinence adviser – 2%

1 = Probation officer – 2%

1 = Ethnic background – 2%

1 = Socialising – 2%

1 = Being away from home area – 2%

1 = Sleeping – 2%

1 = Enough money – 2%

1 = Self – 2%

Medication has helped, but I helped myself as well – I turn away from anger and go somewhere else. When I feel like cutting I make sure I've got nothing in my room.

1 = Nothing – 2%

Nothing's helped – death is the only answer.

CHAPTER 12

Experiences

The service user experiences in this chapter were gathered from responses to the interview questionnaire featured in Chapter 8, with particular reference to Question 6, and also include diary entries from the journals kept by members of the group during the course of the research.

WHEN YOU ARE ABUSED AS A CHILD YOUR LIFE IS MURDERED

Mommie Dearest

My mum has lost all her faith in people and God because of everything that has happened to her and us. She was an abused child – had a terrible childhood – molested, locked in cupboards, kicked, hit, all horrible things, so she has told me, and I can quite believe it, because her mother, my nanna (between you and me) was equally as nasty to me physically and mentally – fucking woman. I was so glad when she died. My mum's father was an alcoholic and Mum says that I remind her of him, when *he* was drunk. I can't tell anyone the next bit that I am so desperate to write about but just can't – yet…I'm going to tell it like it was. When I was young I used to have a shower with her (to save hot water – Dad knew) and in the shower she would wash me with her bare hands, stick her finger up me and would say that I needed to be clean there – free from dirt and bacteria. It was fucking uncomfortable, I can tell you, but at the time I did not realise what it was all about. She would also come into my bedroom during the night and lift up my nightdress and rub and stroke me. I used to pretend I was asleep, but I could feel *everything* that was happening. Mum would *always* want to see my sanitary towels. She was always wanting to see me in just my bra and once I said 'no' and she got really aggressive and said 'Sod you then'. I felt sick with fear. She would also hold me over the toilet and tell me to wee. Sometimes it would not come out and Mum would say 'For God's sake hurry up and go, I can't stand here all day holding you.' Then, if I couldn't go, later I may have wet

99

LIVERPOOL JOHN MOORES UNIVERSITY
LEARNING SERVICES

myself, but God, I didn't tell *her* – I cleared it up myself, or with Dad's help. Neither of us told Mum. She still hugs me, and when we are alone her hands wander down me to my bottom and also to my breasts. She's so clever though – she doesn't do it in public – Dad has seen it, though. I'm 37 years old and basically Mum still has this *hold* over me in more ways than one. When I was about fourteen I tried to poison her with ant poisoner (stuff in a tube). She had wanted me to do her some toast and marmalade. She couldn't taste anything different, all that happened was that she got stomach ache and a bit of diarrhoea. Mum is two people – sweet, loving, kind, caring, and horrible, cruel, sarcastic (very) and abusive. *Yes*, I was abused – I am confused as to whether it was sexual abuse or only molesting. I was (and still am) emotionally and mentally abused and confused and scared by her. But I was only a couple of times ever hit by her, so that is good. Ha! Ha! She didn't need to hit me. Just one look or word put the fear of God in me.

I was abused at home and abused in care. The worst of it was being beaten with a stick in the shower – things like that. But I don't talk about it a lot because saying you're a victim of abuse is like a ticket to sympathy in my book.

The Reunion

I was taken from my pram by my father at an early age. I was abused by my father. After 29 years a letter came from the Salvation Army saying my mother was looking for me. My mum was at the Social Services meeting when I got my little girl back. I now feel I have a family again, although I have lost 29 years with my mum. But, like she says, we have the rest of our lives together. My mum is staying with us at Christmas.

The Lost Children

Today I watched a programme on the television. It was called *The Lost Children* and it was about six girls who were abducted and abused in Belgium by a paedophile, Marc Detroux. Four of the six girls died and two survived. The father of one of the dead girls said the following about his daughter, An Marchal. 'In a way I'm pleased that An is dead. I think, no I'm sure it's better because, when you have to live with such memories I think it's better that you don't live and so I'm sure it's better we didn't find her perhaps alive.' This transcript says it all really and it expresses what I have felt for such a long time. Paul Marchal is obviously a man with real insight into the plight and suffering of victims of child abuse and I agree with what he has said.

No sex, please, no pain,
No hurt, please,
Again…
And again.
Do I ask for that?
Do I need that?
A hoar
A whore,
Cheap and unclean,
Just a continuous
Sex machine.

THE WORLD OF FEELINGS

The Inner Child

I feel so angry, I cannot say it enough times. I feel furious with my 'little girl' and she is enraged with me. I have so much self-loathing inside me. I feel like hiding her, but she was such a lovely, gentle and affectionate little girl it is very difficult to be violent towards her. I don't know what I am going to do with her – she needs so much, but I just want to 'rest in peace'. We have both become very frightened of dying since my last overdose, but I have to be brave for her. How could anyone hurt her so much?

To Whom It May Concern

I'm feeling like I'd like to open up my arms but I have no razor blades with me. (My one saving grace – I had the foresight not to pack any.) I'm not sure how I'm feeling. I'm hearing voices but it's not like before. Before the voices were in my head like thoughts that I had no control over. Now I have more control but the voices seem detached, like one step removed from me. It's a really weird feeling and I don't like it. I wish I could tell someone about this but I don't feel that I can. I feel so isolated and alone. I'm scared of practically everything. That might sound like an exaggeration, but the thought of living, paying bills, coping with people, terrifies me. I know what I should be thinking and feeling, but it's not happening at the moment. I am so scared of losing my kids, but I feel that I am losing my grip on reality.

The Hedgehog

I did the exercise in the book which asks you to think about an animal symbol and this is what I wrote. My animal symbol was a hedgehog and its qualities were that it could hibernate, it had spikes, and that it was quite slow moving. Hedgehogs are nocturnal and this seemed to symbolise my wish to escape everyday life, although I am a bit scared of the dark. Speaking of being nocturnal, it is now 3 a.m. – hedgehogs are also plain, rounded and unattractive and these characteristics symbolise my desire not to be noticed, which is probably why I dress the way I do and that I don't take any care over my appearance. Hedgehogs also hibernate and this symbolises my desire to really escape and huddle up into a little ball to protect myself. The spikes on my hedgehog serve as a form of protection and put people off from handling me, although a soft under-belly does mean that I am still very vulnerable and can easily be badly hurt. Hedgehogs also very often have ticks, which symbolises something sucking at my life force and draining my energy. Finally, hedgehogs are often found in the gutter, dead or badly injured by people in powerful machines, who just hurry on by without a second thought.

Hate

I hate you all, I hate you,
I hate you all like hell,
but I mustn't say it aloud,
I mustn't tell.
I hate that voice,
It will haunt me forever,
I hate his face,
but he's so clever.
There's so much anger inside of me,
I don't know what to do,
I feel afraid, I know one day,
I'll erupt and lash out too.
I've taken my anger out on food and drink,
but a person? I never would dare,
I would hurt them all so very much,
(and secretly I really do care.)
So it's back to the anger,
implanted in my brain,
growing each day – larger than life,
slowly driving me insane.

A Very Confused Poem – written by a very confused person – sorry!

I'm, Jekyll and I'm Hyde,
I've told the truth, and I've also lied.
I'm happy and I'm sad.
I'm good yet also bad.
When I'm Jekyll I can be nice and kind,
but when I'm Hyde I'm horrible you'll find.
When I'm Hyde I look fierce and bad,
I smash things about – I'm insane and mad.
If Jekyll could always be Jekyll
he'd really feel great and high,
but when he's Hyde he's really down
and wishes he could die.
But Hyde cannot kill himself – it's always Hyde he'll be,
Because both Jekyll and Hyde – they really are me.

Who am I now?
PRESTO…Andante
FORTISSIMO…Piano
STACCATO Legato
They're me.

Anger

I COULD EITHER SHOOT OR STAB TO DEATH (WITH A CARVING KNIFE) EVERYBODY IN THIS SO CALLED 'HUMAN RACE', SO THAT I WOULD BE THE ONLY ONE LEFT, APART FROM ALL THE ANIMALS, BIRDS, INSECTS AND NATURE ITSELF. THEN I WOULD BE HAPPY BECAUSE NO ONE COULD HURT ME, LAUGH AT ME, DISBELIEVE ME, SHIT OR URINATE ON ME AND TALK 'DOWN' TO ME. I'VE JUST HAD ENOUGH OF ALL THAT. SO BASICALLY, I WOULD *NEVER* BE TAKEN ADVANTAGE OF *EVER AGAIN*.

I WOULD BE FREE…HAPPY…PEACEFUL…CONTENT…(LOVELY)

SO F… OFF ALL OF YOU.

I have written this all in capital letters because when I am angry I do always write like this. Also, I wrote out fully the obscene language that I used, but I have not done it now because I feel it is inappropriate when researching and explaining my feelings.

Mad, Mad, Mad

Went mad again at football.
I'm mental through and through.
I shouted, I swore, I hit out at things,
I just don't know what to do.
Help me, please, I feel I'm going insane.
Gradually my emotions are destroying my brain.
I can't be calm, however hard I try.
I'm either too 'low', or far too 'high'.
I feel so shaky and I want to smash things about.
If I'm not careful, they'll arrest me as a lout.
I can't control myself, I'm scared of what I might do.
And nobody believes me when I say all this – do you?

Today I started vomiting after meals – it gives me the same sense of control as cutting and is another form of self-harm. It makes me feel as if I can at least control something in my life, even though I have felt quite ill at times, I have also felt a little more settled mentally.

Can't eat – mind won't let me. Took lactulose – chronic diarrhoea. Wish I could go and talk to—. Daren't though. (Paranoid – 'Not *her* back here again. Thought we'd seen the last of her for a good few months, or even years.') Just can't slow down – everything I do is done is fast motion. Oh God, help!

Asleep and half-asleep – throughout the night I was having conversations in my head and answering them out loud, waking myself up. Is this normal? Does everyone have this? Dad is singing in my head 'Summer is a-coming and Mary's getting fat!' So many conversations and talking going on in my head (mostly Mum this time). 'Well, Jack only has a certain time and year left. Every time he talks about the funeral he cries.' (Heard so vividly and clearly in my head.)

5.30 a.m. Mum's voice – 'I'm just going to get the bath clean.'

6.40 a.m. Mum – 'I bit my finger in my room with the wheel and part of the digthry'???

What's it all about? Dad woke me with a jump, me hearing him say angrily – 'Oh Shit'.

Someone with a Personality Disorder can hear voices outside their head. The person thinks that maybe they are schizophrenic. For them that can be slightly easier to cope with and accept because it is recognised and heard of. But hearing your own voice talking to you and telling you what to do, usually compulsive and destructive orders, is phew! Frightening. And also your voice repeats itself, going on and on saying the same words, sentences until you 'obey yourself'. The person gets completely confused, frightened and angry because their own voice is in complete control over their mind and body. It can be my voice in my head saying yes I can – no I can't – yes I can   no I can't – continuously – weird. Loud bangs and knocks and rapping sounds – very scary. It is no wonder that Personality Disorders have not really been recognised or diagnosed because they are so complicated and intricate to comprehend. In the past I have heard other people's voices in my head, usually when I have not been eating properly. Sometimes they were people I knew. Other times it was just a voice that did not make much sense and I was very muddled by it. When asked by doctors if I hear voices I have said no, because it was all so frequent and so constant that, in a way, I thought it was normal and everybody heard them.

Do you know the film *Hell Raiser*? The bloke with all the pins stuck into his head? Well, it's just like that. The pins in his head are all voices and sounds, words from songs I'd listened to during the day, all distorted. They are all constantly turning over and over again and again in my mind and head. They are coming in from each and every direction and I am trying to answer each one all at once – going out of my head – being driven mad.

Silence

I'm distant, vague,
Nothing seems real,
And nothing now
Do I feel.
Silent voices,
Blind visions,
No hopes or dreams,
Plans or missions.
All so quiet…
All so still…
My brain has given up
This struggle up-hill.

Dissociation

Nothing looks real and I cannot appreciate God's creations the way I used to. I went paddling in the sea the other week. I could feel the water on my feet but the emotion was not registering in my head – all my senses feel dead. I feel separate.

I feel really disjointed and somehow out of it – time is really dragging – nothing seems to fit – feel as if I don't belong. I am an outsider looking in. I don't feel part of the world.

I feel so distant all the time and can't remember what I did the day before. I feel I am cracking up physically and mentally. I don't know what is real and what is not. Feel in a kind of dream all the time.

I went to throw something or other in the bin and I saw loads of empty flower-seed packets. I must have planted them somewhere, but I don't know where because I don't recall doing it. I can't remember getting my washing in that I did early in the morning.

No one to phone,
No one at all.
Just no one… no one…
No one to call.
Why? Because you all think
I am attention seeking
Apart from this diary
I'm writing and keeping.

I am writing this letter in an effort to try to stop myself from doing something that others may regret. I continue to feel extremely depressed and I am sick to death of feeling this way and there is a real limit to how much more I can take. We should never have left Essex, I have been offered so little support since we've been here. I so want to just curl up and die, to end this relentless misery once and for all. This existence is really terrible. I feel so isolated and alone.

The Black Hole

The Hole.
The Hell Hole,
A nightmare place
Without a face.
Just black…
Just dark…
Without a mark
Of human race…
No trace.
Not a thing.
Nowhere to cling.
Just nothing…nothing…
Down, down…deeper and deeper…
Steeper and steeper
To climb up again.
No way out…
Can't even shout.
No one will hear,
A place of fear,
And nothing else.
Just a Black Hole,
A Hell Hole…
The nightmare place
Without a face…
Down…down…Helpppppp!

Woman Falls Down Cliff Face (local press)

A major cliff operation was launched after a Colchester woman fell more than 30 ft down a sheer drop at Walton Naze – spotted lying unconscious on a ledge by a member of the public who contacted Thames Coastguard at Walton. He said: 'When I got there the woman was unconscious and around 30–40ft below a sheer drop resting on a ledge – It was a tricky operation as it is the highest point of the cliffs, a sheer drop…'

It's amazing how many people try to kill themselves and fail. I feel that even God does not want me. I feel it's out of my control to bring things to a conclusion. It's very frightening.

No More Tears

There are no tears in heaven,
Just happiness, peace and love,
Gentleness, rest and serenity,
Up in heaven above.

There is no fear in heaven,
No conflicts, struggles or hate,
No anger, pain or confusion,
And no terror, abuse or rapes.

There is no loneliness in heaven,
In Jesus we can confide.
We also have a Guardian Angel,
Who is always by our side.

There is no black in heaven,
We can always see a light,
That shines upon our sad, sad faces
Now so alert, happy and bright.

Heaven is a paradise,
I'd like to book my flight,
But Jesus doesn't want me yet,
So I'll just have to try and fight.

The Reverend has told me that it's all very well and good talking about heaven, but how are you going to get there? Good question!

Bouncing Back

> *Boing! Boing! Bouncing back,*
> *After being driven round the bend.*
> *Tablets, more tablets, cutting, drink,*
> *But again I'm on the mend.*
> *Can't keep going like this, however,*
> *Each time bouncing back.*
> *Sooner or later I'll be tired of this fight,*
> *Sooner or later I'll crack.*

I do have some insight into the causes of my mental state and I also know I can't simply forget the past. I do not live in this hell for the shear fun of it and, if it was possible to move on I would. My whole adult life, and much of my childhood, has been well and truly blighted by what has happened to me. I am a direct product of abusive influences and it is not possible to just wipe away the last 28 years. I genuinely feel that nothing good will ever happen to me, because I seem to go from one disaster and major trauma to the next, but that doesn't mean I don't want things to change.

> *All you people/sufferers out there SPEAK OUT NOW – PLEASE.*
> *I am bursting with the need to write. Every time I stop writing and*
> *look up I am following shapes and counting corners –*
> *Never have I felt so low (solo).*
> *When are you going to get me out of this black hole?*
> *Conversations going on in my head,*
> *Chanting the alphabet – A to Z,*
> *I have to scrub, I have to shower,*
> *To clean myself, I have to scour…*
> *I do TRY and be fine, I really do, but then suddenly I'll flip.*
> *Something happens to me in my head which I CAN'T control or*
> *understand. NO I FUCKING CAN'T. DON'T PRESUME AND*
> *THINK I CAN. I FUCKING CAN'T. (Sorry, I'm swearing. Sorry.)*

I do not want each day and night to be a chore, struggle and trial to get through. I would love to go to sleep at night, looking forward to the following day. I just would not like to have these problems that I do have.

How Do I Cope?

How do I cope with the rest of today?
How do I cope with tomorrow?
How do I cope with starving, then bingeing?
How do I cope with my sorrow?

How do I cope with a racing brain?
How do I cope with talking?
How do I cope with seconds and minutes?
How do I cope with walking?

How do I cope with feeling paranoid?
How do I cope with blinking?
How do I cope with breathing each breath?
How do I cope with thinking?

How do I cope with having bad thoughts?
How do I cope with confusions?
How do I cope with feeling so angry?
How do I cope with illusions?

We make you feel. We also make you suffer. Why? Because in that space after frustration and anger is your desire to wash your hands of us. In a way, we want to make you suffer, because how can there be no answer to this?

Please reach out a helping hand,
Understand.
Talk to me,
Can you not see
How worthless I feel?
How useless I feel?
Unless I get help
I will never heal.

THE THERAPY EXPERIENCE

They put me in the wrong situation. They put me in a group when I specifically told them I don't like group work. I spent 18 months saying nothing.

I have been offered a place on a once-a-week group psychotherapy course lasting up to two years, which I believe is unsuitable for me. I did point out that I didn't believe I could cope in a group and I was told that everyone feels like that at first and that it didn't matter if I didn't talk to the group for a year.

At a women's group we talked about problems. One of the girls had been abused. That upset me. It had a bearing on my own feelings. I changed the subject. Brought my husband into it, saying he annoyed me – talked about my weight.

I go to a support group for survivors of abuse. It's been more helpful for making friends and they understand me a lot because of having a similar background. It gives you coping strategies, but I don't discuss a lot there – I learn from others and their experiences. I only talked about my own experiences with my therapist.

I started a group, substance, tranquilliser and alcohol rehabilitation therapy. That was very good. I talked about panic attacks. I found it helpful to know others are in the same boat.

When I came back from border patrol I was debriefed. We had no counsellor to talk to. We talked about it with other colleagues. We put it down to part of the job.

I had individual music therapy. I felt like a plonker – really inhibited. Music therapy was crap – a waste of time. Inner Child Therapy – there was a lot of writing letters, making things real and having to sign them, and visualisations. I found it difficult but I was happy with this therapy. Cognitive Behavioural Therapy was good. I didn't self-harm for six months. It taught me to distract from my feelings. Also to do relaxation and breathing in the bath. I had CBT while I was waiting for psychotherapy. Psychotherapy didn't help me. It made me worse. I was also at a therapeutic community for three months. It didn't help me. I think it was too soon for that therapy. I wasn't ready.

I got more out of five weeks of CBT than over a year of psychotherapy. Some of it has stayed with me. Sometimes it still helps. But, when my depression falls below a certain level, I can't hang on to the positives.

I get to see a counsellor from NEEDAS (Drug and Alcohol Team) every two weeks. She has started to do CBT. It seems to be helping.

Counselling has been helpful. I've been able to be completely honest in [the voluntary sector] in a way I couldn't be with the services.

A good counsellor can make the difference between life and death.

I cannot believe how two different professionals can come up with two totally different ideas as to the cause of my mental health problems. Of course I trust—. But— simply ignored what did not fit into her theory – my mental health problems stem back to a repressed childhood and basically bad parenting. Worst of all, she dismissed abusive elements from my past – like suffering direct physical, sexual and ritual abuse at the hands of a paedophile ring – by saying they 'didn't seem so real'. I can honestly say I feel as if I have been raped. It's as if she has plundered my very being and soul and rewritten my life history according to what *she* thinks has affected me.

I went to see this person who deals with Inner Child Therapy. The frightening thing is that I do not remember a single word or sentence he or I talked about. I am really frightened by this. The only thing I remember is that I said I would pay him £20 a week.

The Henderson has given me the experience which allows me to understand my past and present behaviour. The Henderson allowed me to be able to confront and be angry with individuals and allow them to be angry with me. This was done in a way that didn't become confrontational or end up in violence. The most important thing was to be able to be in touch with my feelings and own my feelings. It allowed people to give me harsh feedback which was needed or wanted, and allowed me to take on board what people say. It allowed me to be empowered and be responsible for my own actions. It allowed me to recognise that I wasn't alone with this diagnosis. Lastly, by no means do I think this is a cure, a continuation of such therapy must be done. It took a year. I am being treated differently by the psychiatric system now I have done my time in the Henderson. I think they see it as a willingness to look at yourself and take responsibility. One drawback is expectations – illusions really – that the outside world, and continued support, will be as enlightened. It's not. The Henderson is ahead of its time. It doesn't mesh with what comes after, and that can be quite a shock, disempowering. A social worker started to help me, but eventually I took over myself and decided to look for the accommodation and support I need. But that's been a learning experience too.

Psychologist – CAT

You start with 8 or 12 sessions, then 16, but in some cases like my own it can continue without limit of time. It's continued for over two years. I think this depends on how open you are early on – bonding with the therapist – you have more of a chance of making progress. It made me feel worse initially and that's what made me work harder. I've had periods of big ups and downs, usually when I approach a new area. I've had to go into hospital at times to get through the difficult areas. Because you bond so much with your therapist, when they go on holiday it can feel they are running out on you – have relapsed then too. There can be a problem because you have a therapist. When you hit something you need to talk about they say, 'Stop – you need to talk to your therapist about that.' This can happen as an in-patient, out-patient, with the Community Psychiatric Nurse. Even though he's away for two weeks, it may be four weeks until I see him – I've got nobody left – not helpful. In therapy, so far I have identified four different roles I tend to use. I am trying to integrate them into one, into me. I haven't done this yet. I didn't know about them until they were actually found. Now, they are known to me, although they can still take over. I was abused as a kid and after so many sessions I started to get thoughts about being an abuser. It just came up. I mentioned this in confidence to another professional. All the red lights went on – in a big way. Child Protection was involved. I got sectioned – my therapist happened to be on holiday, by the way. It was a nightmare. Everything was going faster than I could take in. I think it should have been contained. It was just a stage I was working through – no need for half the Services to get involved. Nobody is sure what CAT is going to get me in the end. I have changed over the past two years. I understand more. If there was more funding, and more people with experience, I believe there could be an answer to all this. What I want is one whole personality – that's me.

I had psychotherapy. It was terrible. I didn't understand it at all. It was group psychotherapy. I wasn't prepared to talk about what had gone on in my early life. I did it for a year and said nothing. I left the group as it wasn't helping. I had various psychologists, but they usually left before I talked too deeply. I've been to Cognitive Behavioural Therapy, which didn't work. Now in CAT, which is time limited. It's for 24 weeks. I've just started going deep into my past. As I've only got four weeks left, and my therapist has told me she's leaving, I now have to be brought up to coping level, which I think is very unfair because it's the first time I've told anyone about the abuse. The psychiatrist has advised Dialectical Behaviour Therapy – DBT. It's not available in this area yet.

I LOVE MY CHILDREN

Child Protection is a load of bollocks. They take the one thing you have to hold on to and keep you going, without giving you a chance. I felt the social worker was punishing me again after being punished/abused as a child. It made me feel like she was saying – YOU WILL NOT BE HAPPY.

My children are staying with Mum and Dad. The CPN keeps ringing the social worker, who remains elusive, we can't find out what day the meeting takes place on. Now I've had a telephone call from my ex-mother-in-law who says my husband is in a mental hospital himself so he can't look after the children. If they let me keep the children my mum says she'll come over and help me. Otherwise they'll get taken into care if it's decided I can't look after them at the meeting. The social worker is not very helpful. Terrible tangle up. I'm worried that if I go home on the wrong medication I won't be able to look after my kids.

The Child Protection Team failed to offer me adequate support and protection for my children against my ex-husband.

I went to Court and I was not allowed in. I was told 'we are coming for your kids at 5.30 p.m'. I was told this at 4.30 p.m. I am under assessment at the moment. The Orange Book. I am meeting with my kids today. The meeting is supervised and I feel I have to be on my best behaviour all the time. Someone looking over your shoulder all the time. I want my kids back, I will accept any help that can be given.

In 1996 my children were taken away from me. A social worker arrived on my doorstep saying she had received a phone call from a 'friend' stating she was concerned I'd harm the children. Since then my son has remained in the custody of his father, who has a history of violence, and whose parenting abilities have never been assessed by the Local Authority. I did not need 'help' from Social Services on that day. It was forced on me. Previously, when I had asked for assistance, they had placed the children twice at my request. The point being that when I felt I needed help I had always asked for it. I love my children, I would never harm them, and have never self-harmed while they have been in the house. I saw a TV programme about Munchausen's Syndrome by Proxy. It seems it is considered to be a way in which Personality Disordered mothers respond to their children. I wonder if this explains why Social Services were so ready to take away my children.

Social Services intervened. They had it all weighed up before the meetings. They said I was holding the baby like a doll. I asked the social worker at the time if I was doing OK – she told me 'yes, fine'. Then I got the report. It was rubbish. I lost him six months ago.

Child Protection have been the bane of my life. This started with a phone call from my mother-in-law, we think, and resulted in strangers inspecting and picking fault with my home. I know I have been ill and become very upset, but I would never hurt my kids. I took one of my daughters to the GP for a urine infection. She said she suspected sexual abuse and she would have to inform the authorities. I demanded that my daughter see a consultant paediatrician at the General Hospital – that day. I had an advocate present as a witness during the whole proceedings. The consultant found absolutely no evidence of sexual abuse. If it wasn't for the involvement of Social Services with my family, I don't think the possibility of abuse would ever have occurred to the GP.

Mental Health Services wanted me to be admitted on my own. They didn't think I had a suitable problem to be admitted to the mother and baby room. Social Services said I should be admitted to a mother and baby unit. Then the hospital admitted me and my daughter, even though they were reluctant to do so. In the next couple of months I didn't see the special mother and child team it says there was in the leaflet. The doctor said, 'There's nothing wrong with you, you're just miserable.' I was a teenager at the time. I was breast feeding my daughter and they took her away. They said I said I was going to kill her. But I'm sure I didn't. I had a big argument with Social Services because I didn't want my daughter to go to her father who was inexperienced. He took her home. They didn't ask if it was all right. My daughter had been offered a place at the nursery five days a week, but the social worker wanted to take her away instead of trying to work out a way to keep her with me, even though she hadn't been registered on the 'at risk' list. Social Services said it was because I didn't have a proper care plan. They couldn't decide whether she was at risk, although they said she actually appeared to be thriving. After she'd gone home I took an overdose. I threatened to leave and I was sectioned. I had Electroconvulsive Therapy [ECT]. The doctor said he'd try ECT but didn't think it would work and then he decided I might be depressed. Staff were not giving me any support. I was fed up and told nurses I was dying without my child. I went to London for a parenting assessment. It was very good. They did a lot of bonding work with me. I had to fight for months because I hadn't been diagnosed. If I'd had schizophrenia I would have been given immediate treatment.

The Wise Judge

The Report talks about the— children having experienced emotional abuse, well I would not be surprised if they have, but the fact of the matter is that both these parents, however inadequate they are, are the only parents these children have got. The local authority seems to be wanting a Care Order in order to achieve its own ends and transferring the children to Mr—. I know Mr—'s statement and it would seem on the face of it he can barely cope with one child never mind four. It is a perfectly absurd plan. What is more, and I say this so it can be used for whatever purpose anybody likes, it seems to me that whether the local authority's sole purpose in seeking a Care Order is to organise residence in accordance with its wishes, then it seems to me to be verging on an abuse of the process to take care proceedings.

We all have a wonderful notion that we can improve other people's lives. I very much doubt that we can. I am rather inclined to think that we end up with the least worst situation and I do not have any doubt that what I have done here is to provide the least worst situation.

I would add this also. Mrs— is quite patently somewhat fragile. I have seen enough of her to know that she gets easily upset and the thing that upsets her most is the prospect of having her children taken away from her. The local authority might care to think what the effect will be on the children of having proceedings of this kind hanging over the head of Mrs—. They might care to think just where the emotional abuse is coming from.

To say I lack enthusiasm for the local authority's plan is to put it very, very clear indeed. All I can say, looking at the case, on the face of the papers that I have got, however inadequate these parents may be, both of them, they are the only parents these children have got and I see no advantage to them whatsoever in being removed and placed somewhere else. On the contrary, I suspect it would do them a great deal more lasting harm than anything they are likely to suffer at the hands of the parents, who, whatever their faults, do actually love them. There it is. (Court judgement provided with the permission of service user and judge.)

THE SCENARIO OF GREAT FIDELITY

Razor Sharp

Thoughts of the past prominent in my head. Bad person, naughty baby, no wonder my birth mother didn't want me. I'm not deserving of anything good in my life. I need to be punished just because I'm alive. Mind swirling, too many thoughts at once, can't cope. Worthless, burden, angry. The anger is initially directed at the right people. However, it doesn't stay there for long. I soon turn it around and, consequently, the anger returns to me, as it should do, because that's my lot in life. I should be used to it by now. Once more a failure. Get my 'equipment' out, place it in the usual position – razor blades, steristrips, gauze, tape. Sitting in the same chair. Let the battle commence! Fighting a losing battle – need to cut for a release, a short time without the bad thoughts. Physical pain important, as is the bleeding – some of my badness coming out – good. Palpitations begin, trembling, feel sick – definitely losing the battle. Why should I *try not* to cut? What's in it for me? This can go on for anything up to an hour, and I'm trying to distract myself from my thoughts. Relaxation tapes, walk the dog sometimes, hot lavender bath. *Shit* – I've done it. Eight cuts on my forearm, several of them quite deep. Body trembling. Watch the bleeding for a while. Stop the bleeding and take care of the wounds with steristrip and gauze dressing. Shit, it hurts now! Feelings change again. Self-loathing, intense guilt – why did I do it? So the release from thinking was only for a short time – gets shorter each time – but I *still* do it? Tired all of a sudden. Put all equipment away until the next time, because there *is* going to be a next time.

I buy lots of books. Then I rip them up. I buy three or four each week – sometimes more. Books mostly about old England, Dutch grammars, and history. Fifteen or twenty Dutch grammars – twelve to fifteen dictionaries – ripped them all up. Six Dutch bibles. Sixteen or more *Canterbury Tales* and individual 'Canterbury Tales' by the bucketload. It must amount to about a thousand books since I came to England. Sometimes this activity is combined with smashing things up, but not with cutting. I think it stops me from cutting myself more often. I think I do it because, before I came to England, the only thing that helped me survive was drawing strength from my English heritage. When I came to England I was very disappointed. It had become idealised. I feel I must become more English – immerse myself in English culture. Then I feel I should go to

Holland – Dutch books. I feel lost. When I give up, I get out the bibles and the Chaucer and Shakespeare and I rip them all up.

I'm in the wrong garden   the concrete garden – right – no birds singing today. Nowhere to go – no money – no one there – no one cares – feel like a bastard – feel no good – feel like I'm dead – people piss me off during the day – bumping into me – the way they eat – the way they are. Walking the streets – bump into friends I don't know that well – come with us, we'll buy you a drink – have a snort. Then I'm out of it. Bang out of it. They use me – take the piss – laugh at me behind my back – get me to steal things – food – toiletries – clothes – off licence. I get caught. Before I do it I think – going to stay off drugs – going to stay out of trouble with the law. I've got the kind of problems the mental health service doesn't help with. They say – can't handle drugs – I say – can't handle life.

LOCKED UP

I asked for counselling and I was told it's not available in prison. I felt I needed it to face life in prison. I started cutting my arms. I never saw a doctor, only a prison screw put dressing on. I am one of the lucky ones. I came out alive. I saw three people take their own life. All had mental health problems. If you have a mental health problem you don't get any help at all. Prison is not for people with mental health problems of any kind.

In prison I received quite a lot of support after I had been beaten up by the screws. So they put me on section in hospital and I get treated OK.

I've had experiences with quite a few services, from being brought up in care all my child life and then in youth custody centres, also child lock-up centres, mental health hospitals and prison. I found hospital more demeaning than prison, even though it was more relaxing in some ways.

Special Hospital was one of the worst experiences of my entire life. I will never forget it. I was mixed with rapists, murderers, arsonists and paedophiles, and we were expected to get better. The average stay for a woman was eight years. However, I only stayed for one-and-a-quarter years.

I love violent films – Krays – Scum – Texas Chainsaw Massacre. I thought it would be fun to go in prison. You don't know what it's like to be ill treated in prison – to drink water out of the toilet.

Learning Disabilities Secure Unit

I was locked away for four years. They said I had contact with a girl, but nothing happened and now my name is clear. I was locked in a padded cell. If you did something wrong you would be physically beaten. I didn't think I would come out alive. I thought I'd come out in a box.

In prison there was no support at all. Absolutely appalling – hell – horrendous – a lot of the people I met had serious mental health problems or they were drug addicts or alcoholics.

I was in hospital for a bi-polar condition. My diagnosis was changed by a locum psychiatrist. Within a few days I was discharged without money/benefits, medication or proper aftercare, into inadequate accommodation – with so-called 'untreatable Personality Disorder'. I fell into the hands of the police, as I was wandering around Colchester aimlessly, and for two consecutive nights I was held in a police cell because I was so ill. The consultant would not readmit me, either informally or under section. I was taken to court on a harassment charge, in a prison van, in handcuffs, held in the cells beneath the magistrates court. I would have been sent to the remand centre at Holloway Prison if I had not been collected by my parents and sent back on bail to Wales. We made a difficult and dangerous journey in my parents' car. During a break in the journey I was described by a doctor as practically 'psychotic' and 'very manic'. He advised my parents to get me into hospital as soon as possible. When we arrived home I was sectioned and treated as bi-polar, *not* Personality Disordered. Once again, with the right medication and adequate therapeutic support, I gradually became very well again. I find it hard to accept that someone was diagnosed as having a Personality Disorder who was a head girl at school, with good relationships with both parents, obtained the highest qualifications at her school, studied law, history and politics, obtained a good degree with honours and made loyal friends.

I want to kill – think about killing all the time. If I was to kill it would make Hungerford look like a teddy bears' picnic. I make my home my prison.

REFLECTIONS AND SUGGESTIONS

Something is seriously wrong with a system that treats anyone, whatever their education or background, like a 'sinner' or a 'criminal'.

Self-harm is not a diagnosis, it is a symptom of something deeper happening to you. Self-harm is not a suicide attempt but may result in accidental suicide. There are many reasons why people self-harm. What I can say for me, and I believe many other self-harmers, is that self-harming activities are used as a coping mechanism. Some professionals see it as 'acting out' or attention-seeking behaviour. These attitudes are not helpful to self-harmers. Most self-harmers keep their wounds and behaviour secret and they feel too ashamed or embarrassed to tell anybody about it. They are scared of the reaction that they will get from family, friends and professionals.

Isn't it about time professionals started to find out more about the realities of Personality Disorder and the self-destructive torment, frustration and utmost loneliness sufferers go through? Loneliness? Yes, loneliness, because we are so misunderstood, humiliated, desperate, cut-off – the list is endless. Why, oh why don't and won't these professionals and health authorities accept that there is such a condition and illness. Basically I am beginning to realise that they are all possibly too much in denial to acknowledge and accept it. It is said that Personality Disorder cannot be treated. I think it can, with the help of different medications, but most of all by just sitting with us and recognising and trying to understand this condition by listening.

It is no wonder that those of us with a Personality Disorder diagnosis feel like second- or more like third-class citizens (life's rejects). You only have to look at the definitions given in ICD 10 and DSM IV and read comments such as 'limited capacity to express feelings – disregard for social obligations – callous unconcern for others – deviant social behaviour – inconsiderate of others – incompetence – threatening or untrustworthy'. The list is endless, but one thing that these comments have in common is that they are not helpful in any way.

How can the experts really treat us seriously and with any degree of compassion or understanding when they define us as 'attention-seeking' or as 'acting out'? These types of comments do not help and only serve to deepen the distrust we feel and add to our feelings of persecution. As a group we already feel subhuman, threatened, misunderstood and vulnerable, and now we are tarred with the brush of being bad as well as mad. I do believe that subconsciously we pose such a threat that, to some extent, professionals have lost their way. There is no doubt that Personality Disorders are complex and cover many types of behaviours but, together with losing their way, many professionals seem to have lost interest and patience too.

Those of us with Personality Disorder can elicit a negative response and a kind of aloofness from professionals and carers, probably because we are a mass of churning emotions and, unintentionally, this is threatening to others, or stirs up their deep-seated emotions. I think as a nation we British are still too fond of the 'stiff upper lip' and that certain subjects are still very much taboo in this country. Personality Disorder seems to create a similar response to that of bereavement. When a person is bereaved others are slow to get involved, not because they do not care, but because grief stirs up a whole host of feelings and deep emotions in ourselves. Perhaps the severe trauma of someone with a Personality Disorder is able to tap into similar, albeit less intense, but nevertheless overwhelming or threatening emotions.

———————————

I have been thinking about how the staff in general react to the needs of their clients and I firmly believe that in some cases it would be helpful if clients could speak to someone who truly understands how they feel, someone with first-hand experience. I anticipate that this will not go down well with all of the professionals involved in a client's care and I can envisage quite strong opposition. But surely the person who understands best how a suicidal or abuse victim feels is someone who has experienced these feelings and has been in the same situation. I don't mean any service user advocate or a professional, but someone who has had the same or very similar problems.

———————————

What's needed on the wards are abuse counsellors. There is one on one of the wards that I found helpful to talk to. But I found it more difficult to talk to him at first because he is a male nurse. I'm a man, so women might find that even more difficult. This should be available on all wards.

———————————

I do believe that a small specialist unit would be helpful. A sort of crisis intervention unit, perhaps run from a non-hospital setting, i.e. from a house. This unit would only take a small number of victims of childhood abuse, say five, and they would all be female, as would the staff. Obviously a similar unit may need to be set up for male victims, but you would need to discuss that with the people who have more of an insight into male childhood abuse, because it is quite possible that a male unit would need to be staffed by both sexes. As for my suggestions on the female unit, many victims of childhood abuse feel quite threatened by the presence of male staff and clients. Personally, despite having been abused by males and females, whenever I entered hospital it was because I was at crisis level and a risk to myself, but whenever I left it was because I could no longer stand being around so many men, most of whom did not understand how scared and threatened I felt. Somehow to me women pose less of a threat than men, although they are capable of doing just as much damage. It is possible that this type of unit would be even more beneficial to its clients because everyone would have very similar problems and there would be a feeling of solidarity and mutual support.

LIVERPOOL
JOHN MOORES UNIVERSITY
AVRIL ROBARTS LRC
TITHEBARN STREET
LIVERPOOL L2 2ER
TEL 0151 231 4022

A human failing, and one particularly of the medical profession, is that of the need to 'distance/diagnose/categorise/separate'. Perhaps if more people could 'accept/understand/sympathise/not judge', then this world would be a better place. I heard some comment on a children's programme a few weeks ago in which someone said that a man should respect and understand the 'four Bs' of a woman, but this is applicable to all individuals. The 'four Bs' were: respect for a person's background, respect for a person's body, respect and understanding for a person's behaviour and, above all, balance. All I know is that we cannot call ourselves a civilised society when so many people are outcasts and are simply not understood.

CHAPTER 13

The Moral Career of the Client

The wounded inner child is always mystified to some degree. The degree of mystifica-tion depends upon the nature of the abuse the child experienced, the chronicity of abuse, and whether or not there was anyone who did value the child for who they really were. Believing that we are loveable only when we are not being ourself is the result of what I call toxic shame. Toxic shame says that the way you are is not okay, that there is some-thing wrong with you in your very sense of being.

John Bradshaw (1993, p.7)

Irvine Goffman (1961), in his Essays on the Social Situation of Mental Patients and Other Inmates, examined the psychiatric aspect of the 'moral career' of individuals in the context of identity. The 'career' is linked to internal matters such as image of self and external experiences involving rights, social position and life-style. Here lines of development may be followed by studying moral experiences and personal adjustments.

An 'alteration of social fate' (Goffman 1961, p.119) begins for our sample with the revelation that the diagnosis has been conferred. Although our question merely asked how the discovery was made, additional data was volun-teered by many respondents. The reaction to this new-found knowledge includes anger, feeling insulted, blamed, depressed, anxious, daft, abnormal, numb, bewildered, mystified, helpless, shocked and excluded. Of the sample, 20 per cent made this discovery indirectly from records, reports or at Social Services meetings; 14 per cent appeared to consider their Personality Disorder diagnosis to be non-specific. One respondent asked what type it was and was told 'unspecified'. Others appear to have been told about the diagnosis after many years; yet others were told by professionals only after they asked.

Information from respondents highlights the sense of exclusion and hope-lessness connected with disclosure, and gives some sense of the impact this information might have on an individual labouring with the desperately hard task of living with the truth of an early abusive history.

> At the review nobody took time to explain the diagnosis to me and all the discussions took place about me, but not involving me. I remember feeling numb and bewildered, as if everyone knew except me. I felt as if there was little or no hope for me.

> After I was discharged I opened a letter from my psychiatrist to the GP – it said it there. I was a bit stumped – shocked. I'd heard about people that had been diagnosed with Personality Disorder being the black sheep of the community. It made me feel I didn't belong anywhere.

> I'd been through a lot to make me feel bad about myself, but felt I could overcome it. I found out from the psychiatrist's report for a child care case. It was the first time I knew. It made me feel very low about myself – helpless.

Of the sample, 26 per cent claim not to know what the diagnosis means. A further 22 per cent feel they have been given the diagnosis when professionals 'can't treat or figure out what's wrong with you'. Goffman (1963) considers that a significant phase in a moral career is the point at which an individual discovers that he or she possesses a particular stigma and learns the consequences of possessing it. This can establish important patterns for development. The sample shows that, whether or not they are cognisant of the meaning given by psychiatry to the term 'Personality Disorder', they are largely aware of its pejorative connotations.

> It is no wonder that those of us with a Personality Disorder diagnosis feel like second-, or more like third-class citizens (life's rejects). You only have to look at the definitions given in ICD 10 and DSM IV and read comments such as 'limited capacity to express feelings – disregard for social obligations – callous unconcern for others – deviant social behaviour – inconsiderate of others – incompetence – threatening or untrustworthy'. The list is endless, but one thing that these comments have in common is that they are not helpful in any way.

Responses corroborate the description of the diagnosis as having maximum stigma effect and minimum therapeutic value (Pilgrim 1991). This may explain why consultant psychiatrists, who were very co-operative with our study in other ways, volunteered so few of their patients as respondents. It appears likely that some service users may have been unaware that they had this diagnosis. Consultants may also have questioned the wisdom of focusing attention on the

label of 'Personality Disorder', in light of its stigmatising nature. This consti-
tutes a serious information problem and is an obstacle to telling people much
more relevant and accurate information.

Seventy-two per cent of the sample consider they have experienced bad
treatment because of the label. Confirming that the diagnosis is stigmatising,
respondents describe exclusion in terms of: services leper; wide-berth; you're
ignored; hostility; not mental illness; brought on oneself; people seem to be
scared of the diagnosis; it is saying troublemaker. One respondent considered
that she ended up in a top security hospital because mental illness went unrecognised for approximately six years. Another describes her brief acquaintance
with the diagnosis in an interlude between her more usual classification of
bi-polar disorder. This resulted in discharge from hospital and a highly inappropriate encounter with the criminal justice system. Although other accounts
are less sensational, they reflect a counterpoint of accustomed rejection and
desired engagement.

Of the survey respondents, 38 per cent have experienced imprisonment.
This study is not drawing conclusions about the implications of the diagnosis
in relation to criminal justice disposal, other than to offer experiential reflections.

> I'm confused – can't get a job because of my prison record – my mum
> doesn't want to help me – I damage things – have lost my temper with
> guns and knives – told I can't be helped.

> Before I do it I think – going to stay off drugs   going to stay out of trouble
> with the law. I've got the kind of problems the mental health service
> doesn't help with. They say – can't handle drugs – I say – can't handle life.

The Reed Report (1992) recommended that mentally disordered offenders
should be cared for and treated by health and social services rather than in the
criminal justice system. The report suggested community rather than institutional settings, security no greater than justified, near homes and families, and
support which would maximise rehabilitation. Its recommendation regarding
Court Diversion Schemes has resulted locally in the creation of a Criminal
Justice Mental Health Team (CJMHT). A percentage analysis of support shows
that 42 per cent of the sample experienced help from such a team. Appreciation
is divided fairly equally in terms of finding the service helpful or not. A conclusion here might be that the advantages of such a function can be restricted by
the quality of associated services. A CJMHT, lacking access to a local forensic
psychiatrist, being subject to the unavailability of alternative remand options,

and being further hampered by community services which include high case-load community psychiatric nurses and social workers, may be judged to be only as good as its attendant services. The hinterland that those with this diagnosis tend to inhabit in terms of psychiatric legitimacy, and the fact that such a categorisation may precipitate a reluctance on the part of professionals to engage, suggests an increase in the likelihood that a prison experience might become part of the moral career of those who have attracted a diagnosis of Personality Disorder. The inappropriateness of prison has been described by respondents.

> In prison there was no support at all. Absolutely appalling – hell – horrendous – a lot of the people I met had serious mental health problems.

> I am one of the lucky ones. I came out alive. I saw three people take their own life. All had mental health problems. If you have a mental health problem you don't get any help at all. Prison is not for people with mental health problems of any kind.

Child protection experiences were also highlighted within the study. The current requirement of the State to protect children from abuse is not something which is in question; nor is the fact that there may be circumstances in which it is justified to remove a child to safety. However, of the 30 per cent of respondents in our sample who had experienced child protection social workers, 67 per cent considered the experience to have been harmful. This is the highest harmful rating percentage amongst 25 possible interventions, higher even than the armed forces. Goffman (1963) considers that those with an 'inborn' stigma may become socialised into a disadvantaged position even when they are trying to incorporate standards in society against which they fall short. An inability to reach those standards can cause a terrible compounding and confirmation of internal perceived inadequacies.

> I felt the social worker was punishing me again after being punished/abused as a child. It make me feel like she was saying, *you will not be happy*.

> I am so scared of losing my kids, but I feel I am losing my grip on reality.

> I'm worried that if I go home on the wrong medication, I won't be able to look after my kids.

> I was breast-feeding my daughter and they took her away – after she'd gone home I took an overdose. I threatened to leave and I was sectioned. I had ECT – I told nurses I was dying without my child.

The Children Act 1989, was based on guidance and regulations made explicit in the White Paper preceding its publication.

> There are unique advantages for children in experiencing normal family life in their own birth family and every effort should be made to preserve the child's home and family links. A wide variety of services, including short-term out of home placement, may need to be employed in order to sustain some families through difficult periods. The provision of services to help maintain the family home is a requirement of the Children Act 1989. (DoH 1989 ch. 2, para. 2)

Loss of their children has, at some time, been experienced by 38 per cent of our sample. Others live in constant fear that they may be taken from them at any moment.

> Mrs— is quite patently somewhat fragile. I have seen enough of her to know that she gets easily upset and the thing that upsets her most is the prospect of having her children taken away from her. The local authority might care to think what the effect will be on the children of having proceedings of this kind hanging over the head of Mrs—. They might care to think just where the emotional abuse is coming from. (Excerpt from Court judgement)

Hunt (1988, p.66) speaks of parents feeling 'isolated, marginalized and powerless throughout the investigative process'. Aldgate and Tunstill (1995, p.38), in their investigations of the implementation of Section 17 of the Children Act, discovered a social worker who commented, 'We are just police. It's no wonder the public doesn't like social workers. I can see the need to follow up families after investigation but we are not allowed to do so. It's all statutory work'.

Why should many actions by child protection services be so inconsistent with the spirit of the Children Act? Hunt (1998) considers that when a government agency undertakes intrusive actions in the line of duty, it must establish accountability for those actions. He concludes that there has been a failure in such accountability which includes a lack of strategic management at government level. Why are children and parents, who have been traumatised by investigatory procedures, not identified by authorities and assessed for need, then afforded help to put their lives together again? Chronic underresourcing of social work departments has reached such crisis levels nationally that South African social workers have been imported to man social work teams in Essex. Resource constraints appear to push the focus of action into protection issues.

Do staff constraints within these areas also make those with mental health problems, particularly those with a diagnosis of Personality Disorder, an easily identifiable target for investigation?

> I saw a TV programme about Munchausen's Syndrome by Proxy. It seems it is considered to be a way in which Personality Disordered mothers respond to their children. I wonder if this explains why Social Services were so ready to take away my children.

> I've been treated like I'm a mad person, instead of an ill parent or disabled person. I'm treated like I'm not trying hard enough.

A refreshing exception to the rule was reported by one respondent in our study suggesting a spirit of co-operation which was probably of great benefit to both mother and child. 'Foster and day care – helped me to be able to look after my own needs.' However, the high 'harmful' rating emerging in relation to child protection social workers indicates that there is likely to be a lack of trust between parents and Social Services.

> I did not need 'help' from Social Services on that day. It was forced on me. Previously, when I had asked for assistance, they had placed the children twice at my request, the point being that when I felt I needed help I had always asked for it.

> On my initial introduction to the family Mrs— presented as hostile towards me, stating that she would not co-operate with anyone from the department. Mrs— made it clear that she did not like or trust social workers and that I was no different from previous workers that she had known. (Excerpt from social worker's assessment, November 1999, provided by respondent)

There appears to be a function here which falls between two services. This involves the blending of the needs of the parent and the needs of the child. Parents in our sample appear to consider that those needs are not in conflict to the degree that Social Services considers them to be. Trust may be so damaged, and subsequent complaints have been so ineffective, that parents might consider an independent support function which bridges services to be the most acceptable: 'A specialist Centre for parents with mental health problems.' Such projects do exist. The Bridge Project was set up by a mental health social worker and is now run by the voluntary sector. It provides respite care, activities for parents and children and help in the home for families who have a parent with mental health problems (Diggins 2000).

Child protection services may represent themselves as an agency that is engaged in interrupting the cycle of abuse. Transgenerational trauma may become transmitted to a second generation (Fonagy 1999). Such an example is explicitly described by a respondent at the beginning of Chapter 12. However, Bowlby (1988) identifies that an adverse effect on personality development might be caused not just by inadequate maternal care in childhood but also by separation of children from those they know and love. The potential negative outcome of growing up in care is well documented (DoH and SS 1985; DoH 1991). For such reasons the Children Act has been created to emphasise retention and support of the family group wherever possible.

> To say I lack enthusiasm for the local authority's plan is to put it very, very clear indeed. All I can say, looking at the case, on the face of the papers that I have got, however inadequate these parents may be, both of them, they are the only parents these children have got and I see no advantage to them whatsoever in being removed and placed somewhere else. On the contrary, I suspect it would do them a great deal more lasting harm than anything they are likely to suffer at the hands of the parents, who, whatever their faults, do actually love them.' (Excerpt from Court judgement)

Hunt (1998, p.3) points out that the potential harmful effects of getting things wrong are as grave and damaging within Social Services as they are within medicine or the judicial system. He argues that this area suffers from similar problems because 'they have similar outmoded cultures, structures and processes. They are hierarchical, they exclude significant stakeholders, they have introverted and sometimes arcane discourses and perceptions and they are secretive and defensive.'

Findings suggest that the moral careers of clients in our study have included both stigma and the violation of rights. Whilst engaged in the construction of the questionnaire, our research group registered difficulty with the concept of a question in the interview schedule which asked about strengths. Their concern was that they might not be able to identify any personal strengths. This indicates that strengths may be a particularly difficult focus for this client group. Nevertheless, during the actual study, only 12 per cent of our sample were unable to talk about strengths. However, rather than building on strengths, in the context of identity their experiences within the system have resulted in personal adjustments in the perception of self which include: not belonging; black sheep; hopeless case, separate; a loner; no confidence;

abnormal; threatened; self-loathing; attention seeking; misunderstood; subhuman; trouble maker; untreatable; no good; a burden; undeserving; worthless; bad parent; bad. This proposes a clue to the quality of depression which might be experienced by this client group, which can be integrally associated with low self-esteem and a distorted sense of self. These internal perceptions might also be interpreted as a reconfirmation of all the messages received by a child subject to early abuse.

CHAPTER 14

The Diagnostic Straitjacket

The current categorical diagnoses of personality disorder, although these are now well known to most clinicians, mainly because of the well-oiled publicity that always accompanies a new edition of the Diagnostic and Statistical Manual of Mental Disorder *(DSM), in the current language of medical science, have little evidence base.*

Peter Tyrer (2000, p.22)

During the mid-nineteenth century, for the sake of their asylum statistics, doctors worked with a few obvious categories of diagnosis, such as melancholia, general paralysis of the insane and dementia (Shorter 1997). In the early twentieth century the American census contributed greater reflectiveness regarding diagnosis and, in 1918, the first *Statistical Manual for the Use of Institutions for the Insane* was published (National Committee for Mental Hygiene 1918). The requirements of health insurance in the USA called for the legitimisation of diagnostic classifications and, in 1952, the first *Diagnostic and Statistical Manual of Mental Disorders* (DSM) was born. In a pharmaceutical industry which is second only in productivity to the international arms industry a professional statistical manual of classification and diagnosis simplifies research and sales (Rowe 1997). However, agreements amongst professionals do not always reflect reality, and a model of the mind defined in terms of disease does not necessarily reflect how we think, feel and behave.

In 1999, Kutchins and Kirk published their close examination of the circumstances surrounding the update of the American diagnostic manual in 1987, DSM III. The American Psychiatric Association appointed a work group consisting of eight psychiatrists. Although comprehensive participation was invited, including 25 advisory committees and over 250 consultants, this wider involvement was restricted in that major decisions and modifications were made by the work group. In excess of 200 categories existed; over half of these were changed and over 30 new categories were added, which were to include two new Personality Disorder classifications. These changes were accepted without dispute until a group of feminist psychotherapists seriously challenged the American Psychiatric Association regarding the implications for women in relation to three of the new inclusions, Paraphilic Rapism, Premenstrual Dysphoric Disorder, and Masochistic Personality Disorder. In revising DSM III (1987), research psychiatrists claimed great scientific achievements in classification, yet the work group had failed to subject their revisions to field trials or tests for reliability.

Diagnostic themes relevant to reliability might include an understanding of the genus of Personality Disorder. The nature/nurture debate contains little genetic research. Danish studies of Antisocial Personality Disorder in the twin population revealed that in 36 per cent of identical twins the diagnosis concurred, while in non-identical twins this was 12 per cent (Christiansen 1970). However, in most other twin studies the differences for Personality Disorder are not as significant and, by comparison with other mental disorders, the genetic predisposition appears to be low (Tyrer 2000). Definitions of temperament and personality may become interchangeable but Rutter (1987) suggests that personality involves habitual cognitive processes and motivational traits that move beyond the dispositional characteristics of temperament. Although Tyrer does not necessarily argue a distinction between temperament and Personality Disorder, he concedes that evidence from genetic, clinical and follow-up studies of Personality Disorder are more complex than temperament and involve a range of environmental influences. This concession opens the door to a continued debate about the origins of Personality Disorder, one which this study would argue is significantly influenced by early trauma.

DSM IV (1994) and ICD 10 (1992) represent the current psychiatric preference for the categorical diagnosis of Personality Disorder. Here the clinician is not concerned with recording the clinical features and symptoms of mental illness but rather with assessing how maladaptive behaviour affects self and others. In our study, respondents reveal their awareness of this classification as not so much a diagnosis, but as a poorly adapted coping mechanism.

Self-harm helps as this is a way of coping. If I didn't self-harm I'd be more suicidal.

Today I started vomiting after meals – it gives me the same sense of control as cutting.

No one there – no one cares – feel like a bastard – feel no good – feel like I'm dead…steal things… Before I do it I think – going to stay off drugs –

going to stay out of trouble... They say – can't handle drugs – I say – can't handle life.

Need to cut for a release, a short time without the bad thoughts. Physical pain is important, as is the bleeding – some of my badness coming out – good.

Self-harm is not a diagnosis, it is a symptom of something deeper happening to you... What I can say for me, and I believe many other self-harmers, is that self-harming activities are used as a coping mechanism. Some professionals see it as 'acting out' or attention-seeking behaviour. These attitudes are not helpful to self-harmers.

While assessment of risk remains a necessary component of diagnosis, a classification of Personality Disorder can be conferred as a reaction to perceived risk. Service users have described the experience of being labelled with what they consider to be a pejorative diagnosis. Here they have contributed their thoughts to the moral versus the healing discourse.

You're not seen as a human being but as a diagnosis.

It's hands off – give her a wide berth.

I felt I was given a label that implied it was my fault.

It's either secure hospital or no support at all.

Bad and evil – born with your personality.

Life sentence – untreatable – no hope.

Something is seriously wrong with a system that treats anyone, whatever their education or background, like a 'sinner' or a 'criminal'.

Diagnostic manuals define the disorder in terms of deficiency.

Lack the ability to maintain personal relationships. (DSM IV 1994)

Intense inappropriate anger. (DSM IV 1994)

Frantically try to avoid abandonment. (DSM IV 1994)

Excessive efforts to avoid abandonment and a series of suicidal threats or acts of self-harm, although these may occur without obvious precipitants. (ICD 10 1992)

Show no remorse for their behaviour. (DSM IV 1994)

Callous unconcern for the feelings of others. (ICD 10 1992)

Marked proneness to blame others. (ICD 10 1992)

Incapacity to feel guilt. (ICD 10 1992)

Respondents describe experiences in terms of self-blame and precipitants. Their descriptions encompass context rather than pervasive or enduring behaviour. Some aspirations include compassion and the desire to change.

I need to be punished just because I'm alive.

Feel no good.

Filled with guilt.

I couldn't forgive myself for past events in my life.

Things that have gone on in my life since being a little girl.

You're affected in early life – like a computer with some data missing.

Only one personality is accepted – the adult.

The Inner Child – I don't know what I am going to do with her – she needs so much, but I just want to 'rest in peace'. We have both become very frightened of dying since my last overdose, but I have to be brave for her. How could anyone hurt her so much?

> I'm Jekyll and I'm Hyde,
> I've told the truth, and I've also lied.
> I'm happy and I'm sad,
> I'm good, yet also bad.

I could either shoot or stab to death everybody in this so-called human race...then I would be happy because no one could hurt me, shit or urinate on me...I would never be taken advantage of ever again.

My whole adult life, and much of my childhood, has been well and truly blighted ...I am a direct product of abusive influences and it is not possible to just wipe away the last 28 years...but that doesn't mean I don't want things to change.

I think I have strong compassion.

Deep down I am a caring person. I try to help people in my own way.

Determined to get better, artistic and willing to change.

To be given another chance in life, that's all I ask.

Clinical descriptions observe from the outside, and are surface perceptions of feelings and behaviour.

Disturbed self image. (ICD10 1992)

Attention seeking in various contexts. (DSM IV 1994)

Low frustration tolerance. (ICD 10 1992)

Disregard for violation of rights of others. (DSM IV 1994)

Unstable affects and impulsivity. (DSM IV 1994)

Self-destructive behaviour. (ICD 10 1992)

The experience of respondents paints a profoundly subjective picture that describes early events and feelings associated with dysfunctional behaviour. The sense of self is explored in terms of symptomatology which includes dissociative states and hearing voices. Voices are not described in a form akin to a diagnosis of schizophrenia, where sometimes the television or radio may be perceived as broadcasting personalised messages or where a microphone believed to be in the ceiling might give directions. Here voices may be one's own voice or the voice of another, heard internally or externally and experienced as controlling or defamatory.

The quality of depression is expressed in relation to rejection, isolation and low self-esteem or unworthiness.

My mind and body are separate. I'm angry and disappointed and not able to cope.

I feel so distant all the time and can't remember what I did the day before. Feel I am cracking up physically and mentally. I don't know what is real and what is not. Feel in a kind of dream all the time.

Someone with a Personality Disorder can hear voices outside their head…hearing your own voice talking to you and telling you what to do, usually compulsive and destructive orders, is phew! Frightening.

Throughout the night I was having conversations in my head and answering them out loud, waking myself up. Is this normal? Does everyone have this?

A nightmare place… Without a face… Down… Down… Helppppp…!

I get depressed – thoughts of self-harm and harming others – the voices are terrifying – at times there's no control – desperate – a loner.

Feel unable to cope with the stresses of life – let people wind me up – anxiety – bottled up feelings – fear of rejection – problems stem from childhood.

Very depressed – useless – worthless – no self-esteem or confidence – no hope – I have been crushed by the past.

In a climate where a diagnosis of Personality Disorder suggests inflexible deficits, where prognosis is still viewed with pessimism and treatability remains a thorny issue, respondents in this study highlight inadequate service provision and response, and give clues to the alleviation of their difficulties and potential healing.

General unwillingness to help – refused treatment.

Told there was nothing wrong with me – I banged my fists against the wall and he threatened to call the police.

Treated less sympathetically – not mental illness – something you have brought on yourself.

I've been treated very unfairly – so rudely – without respect – like an idiot.

A human failing, and one particularly of the medical profession, is that of the need to distance/diagnose/categorise/separate. Perhaps if more people could accept/understand/empathise/not judge, then this world would be a better place… All I know is that we cannot call ourselves a civilised society when so many people are outcasts and are simply not understood.

You're ignored – people can be hostile – you're not taken seriously. People don't believe there's anything wrong with you if you've got Personality Disorder.

There's two groups of people, those who try to understand and those who think you're just attention seeking and you don't deserve treatment.

It was a long time before I was properly treated. Lived everywhere – I was in the night shelter – picked up in a nunnery – got medication sorted in hospital and good accommodation – been well for four years.

To be listened to and respected and not to have my pain ignored and unheld.

More talking to find deep-rooted problems.

People fixate on self-harm. They need to look at why people self-harm – need to be looked at as a whole person not just a collection of symptoms.

Crisis house, crisis team, more out-of-hours support.

I do believe that a small specialist unit would be helpful. A sort of crisis intervention unit, perhaps run from a non-hospital setting, i.e. from a house.

A specialist centre for parents.

People understanding – better forms of treatment.

What's needed on the wards is abuse counsellors.

One guideline for everybody so nobody gets confused.

Get rid of the Personality Disorder label.

Terminology rephrased and brought up to date.

Psychological help – been there for me – given me support and counselling – been what I've needed over the past couple of years.

Help with the practical stuff.

Encouragement and support.

The right kind of supported accommodation.

Homestart helped with the kids – taking them out – general support.

Writing, music and being able to express myself.

College boosted my confidence – challenging – energising – given me a purpose – treated more like a human being.

Specifically told them I didn't like group work. I spent eighteen months saying nothing.

A good counsellor can make the difference between life and death.

The Henderson has given me the experience which allows me to understand my past and present behaviour.

In CAT – it's for 24 weeks – now have to be brought up to coping level, which I think is very unfair because it's the first time I've told anyone about the abuse.

CAT – I've seen him for over a year. He's done more than the whole services put together.

I would love to go to sleep at night looking forward to the following day.

What I want is one whole personality – that's me.

A significant question in the diagnostic debate is whether it is possible to separate Personality Disorder from mental illness. Tyrer (2000) considers that it has helped significantly to have Personality Disorder evaluated separately but that it is less well described by classifications than other types of mental disorder because the degree of overlap between categories is so great. Co-morbidity between Personality Disorder subclassifications is evident in our study and the percentage analysis of selected themes in Table 10.11 shows that, regardless of whether the diagnosis is Borderline or Dissocial, early experience of traumatic events and harm to self and others is evident across categories.

Co-morbidity between Personality Disorder and mental illness also proves itself to be difficult to distinguish in the study. High incidences of depression at 78 per cent and anxiety at 60 per cent are shown in Table 10.8 and Figure 10.1. However, the quality of depression is associated with low self-esteem, guilt and a distorted sense of self. High levels of anxiety created by minor stresses appear to be the result of individuals who are emotionally vulnerable to revictimisation growing up in an invalidating environment (Linehan 1999; Van der Kolk 1996).

Depression – my mind doesn't work – I feel anxious all the time.

Suffering the effects of being sexually abused as a child – depression – panic – bulimia – don't belong – anxiety – stress – insomnia – self-harm.

Incidences of a diagnosis of Personality Disorder combined with manic depression or schizophrenia are lower but also significant at 22 per cent and 14 per cent respectively. I recall two service users from our study pondering the fact that they considered their symptoms to be identical, yet one had received an additional diagnosis of schizophrenia and one had not.

Someone with a Personality Disorder diagnosis can hear voices outside their head. The person thinks maybe they are schizophrenic. For them that can be easier to cope with because it is a diagnosis that is accepted because it is recognised and heard of.

They said I didn't have a psychotic episode when I was screaming at voices.

Bi-polar symptomatology was also evident for some who had not received a secondary diagnosis of manic depression.

> *Help me please I feel I'm going insane.*
> *Gradually my emotions are destroying my brain.*
> *I can't be calm however hard I try.*
> *I'm either too low or far too high.*

Either too high or too low – I've heard voices and experienced visual hallucinations and I have a bad temper. I have tried to kill myself – cut and taken overdoses. I've also tried to set light to my head.

Severe and unresolved trauma does appear sometimes to result in dissociative states followed by psychotic-type episodes. A complex interrelationship can exist between traumas, neglect, attachment patterns, and environmental and mental chaos (Van der Kolk 1996). Therefore, in such contexts, should a diagnostic category or trait classification be sought, or should a postmodern approach to diagnosis be negotiated with service users? This would be an interpretive approach to diagnosis, one which does not attempt to fit the client into a category but rather might help them to make sense of their experiences and symptoms (Bracken and Thomas 2000).

The categorical approach to diagnosis, however, currently remains the preferred option and, as a poor measure, this may become influenced by the subjective judgement of the clinician. Yet assessment of personality difficulties by dimension has been in existence longer than diagnostic subcategorisation. Clark and Livesley (1996) argue for a dimensional system and against categorisation because they believe the latter is unreliable and non-specific, and the ability to separate Personality Disorder from mental illness is difficult. They advocate replacing categorical classification by a set of higher- and lower-order dimensional characteristics.

A number of instruments exist for the dimensional assessment of personality difficulties. Some follow DSM categories but measure the level of associated distress, some measure the dimensions of extraversion, neuroticism and psychoticism (Eysenck 1975) and, more unusually, the Karolinska Psychodynamic Profile measures the psychodynamic aspects of personality and can be used to monitor changes over the course of therapy (Weinryb, Gustavasson and Rossel 1997). The Hare Psychopathy Checklist measures the concept of psychopathy both categorically and dimensionally. Standard features include glibness, superficial charm, self-grandiosity, risk-taking behaviours, lying, lack of guilt, callousness, insensitivity, impulsiveness, promiscuity and irresponsibility (Hare 1991). It encompasses the notion that psychopathy is different from Antisocial Personality Disorder.

> It is no wonder that those of us with a Personality Disorder diagnosis feel like second, or more like third-class citizens... As a group we already feel subhuman, threatened, misunderstood and vulnerable, and now we are tarred with the brush of being bad as well as mad... You only have to look at the definitions...the list is endless, but one thing that these comments have in common is that they are not helpful in any way.

Clark and Livesley (1996) believe that dimensional assessment helps to destigmatise; however, such a system may breed a different order of difficulties. Although no actual psychiatric classification exists for Severe Personality Disorder, this notion is used widely by clinicians, especially in the forensic arena. It is considered that Severely Personality Disordered people have overlapping or co-morbid Personality Disorder diagnoses (Oldham, Skodol and Kellman 1992). The Personality Disorder Assessment Schedule of ICD 10 assesses the number of traits and their impact on social functioning. Such impact tends to encompass the notion of risk assessment and opens the door to the concept of Dangerous Severe Personality Disorder (DoH 1999a). Peter Oats (2002, p.2), former Chair of the Patients' Council at Broadmoor Hospital, suggests:

We can surely do without the 'dangerous' tag. Severe Personality Disorder speaks volumes enough... Apart from scaring those even more who suffer from Personality Disorder, not to mention the public, it is in my view nothing more than a waste of finance and an even further drain on mental health services and resources. One hundred and twenty million pounds would better be spent in two ways. Firstly on local mental health services and secondly going into primary and secondary schools to do better research with early warnings of Personality Disorder. Surely the whole aim is not only to prevent children growing up with severe forms of Personality Disorder, but also to help prevent them entering the criminal justice system as an offender.

Although the claim here is not that the diagnostic and statistical manuals have been developed totally without field trials for reliability, their classification system does, however, have a strong flavour of psychiatrists holding up their hands to vote. Additionally, the work of the trait psychologists is considered by Tyrer (2000) to include too many assessment schedules in the diagnostic kitchen. In contrast, psychodynamic influences on personality classification are accused of being confusing, difficult to integrate, and lacking in research evidence. However, it is suggested by this study that psychodynamic attachment theories hold the key to a fundamental understanding of this condition (Bowlby 1988; Fonagy 1997). Brushing aside vast complexity, here service users are simply suggesting that this diagnosis is, if anything, about *harm*. It is about those who have been harmed, usually in childhood, who grow up to harm themselves or others.

It has been argued that all forms of the categorisation of Personality Disorder be abandoned in favour of a global concept (Rutter 1987). The Henderson Hospital has indeed worked with a generic notion of Personality Disorder for some decades. The Henderson network is currently working with a redefinition of Personality Disorder which includes 'those who have histories of emotional, interpersonal and behavioural difficulties which may have been expressed through impulsive, violent and self-harming behaviour'.

In relation to the diagnostic debate, we believe our study has highlighted the multifaceted meaning of Personality Disorder and, in particular, how this varies between professionals and those who hold the diagnosis. There are clear indications that the diagnosis of Personality Disorder and its subcategories represent an intellectual straitjacket that endures out of tradition rather than scientific accuracy. It is fundamentally flawed because it fails to capture the experience of the sufferer.

CHAPTER 15

Spreading the Word

The first great commandment is, don't let them scare you.

Elmer Davis (1954)

At a conference called 'Personality Disorder, who is responsible?' (London, June 1999), the Home Office spoke about preventative detention for approximately 380 individuals. The conference programme for the day listed the last entry as 'Service users' views'. Two service users gave their views. They both had a diagnosis of manic depression. It was most obvious that the view of a major stakeholder, the service user with a diagnosis of Personality Disorder, was not being included. However, in October 2000 we were invited to present the results of our research at a follow-up conference entitled 'Public Protection'. By this time we had spoken at a number of local and national conferences.

Early in 2000 the first opportunity arose to present the results of the research. This came as a request from Professor Shulamit Ramon to talk about the study to PhD students at Anglia Polytechnic University. A day or two before the appointment Shula just happened to mention that I would be conducting this seminar with Professor David Pilgrim. The research report was not quite completed and, on the day, I set out for the Chelmsford site of the university with far too many overhead acetates and feeling a certain sense of anxiety regarding my ability to co-present effectively with David Pilgrim. On my arrival I discovered that the seminar was split between two sites by the use of a video link, that horror of horrors. David Pilgrim, Shula and half the class smiled at me by video monitor from the Cambridge site. I sat in Chelmsford with the other half of the class and nervously sifted through my overheads. However, our results were well received, provoked lively discussion, and even elicited comments about the importance of the research.

For me, the most valuable part of the afternoon was to hear David Pilgrim's discourse on 'construct validity'. This had great relevance to the discussion of our results in relation to the diagnostic debate covered in the preceding chapter.

David pointed out that a subject with poor conceptual validity has the potential to undermine a research study about it. He proposed that the personality trait theory presents a discontinuity and variability in diagnoses. Causes are contested because there is an absence of aetiological specificity. Definitions lack an independent reference point. Meanings become circular. Someone self-harms, or displays antisocial behaviour, therefore they have a Personality Disorder. Because someone has a Personality Disorder they self-harm or display dissocial behaviour. The diagnosis is an elastic concept which may include a wide range of people and encompass a variety of presentations. DSM IV and ICD 10 definitions suggest that those with this diagnosis may display certain behaviours or embody certain character traits. But these definitions do not say why. David pointed out that such contested validity might, to some degree, be applied to other DSM IV (1994) and ICD 10 (1992) diagnoses, but that the classification of Personality Disorder in particular is everything that mental illness is not within the discourse of psychiatry. He questioned how can a research study overcome such a conundrum? Although this label lacks context, and has dubious validity, it does have a living meaning within services. It may have a different meaning within the field of psychology, where discourses between personality development and personality theory have been more closely examined. He concurred with our study that, within psychiatry, beliefs that a condition is negatively enduring can be stigmatising and the context may become *risk*. However, he asked, if such a classification should come to be demedicalised, without the diagnosis would individuals become ignored or criminalised?

Giving consideration to David Pilgrim's thoughts on research construct, I reflected on the fact that 'new constructs' can emerge in the lay arena (Coulter 1973). The Dutch psychiatrist, Marius Romme, examined the subject of voices from the sufferers' perspective (Romme and Escher 1993). His discoveries included the fact that one-quarter of the people who hear voices have never been in contact with psychiatric services. This exploration of experiential knowledge is a reformulation of what 'hearing voices' means. Such reformulations might inform policy and practice. Fransella (1990) points out that we make ourselves prisoners by the way we construe things. If Personality Disorder has a weak context, it will encourage thinking out of context. Kelly (1986) suggests that researchers should start, not with theories, but with involvement in the life situation of people they have chosen to study. The aim of research should be a collaborative exploration to gain an insider's view of reality. Here people are responded to as complex beings rather than reduced to numerical variables. What we had achieved in our research, by attempting to create a new construct from *within* (Freire 1970), was one answer to the conundrum of researching a subject with poor validity.

Soon after this PhD seminar Shula was to arrange our first public presentation of the research at the National Institute of Social Work in London. Two service users agreed to accompany me. They had both acted as interviewers during our study and had major involvement with the research. Karen felt far from well that day, and Linda had hurt her foot and arrived on crutches. Great excitement at Colchester railway station when the stair lift had to be utilised for Linda. We had never seen it in operation before. We arrived in London, did the circuit of Tavistock Square, crutches and all, and eventually found the Institute. Not to outdo herself in relation to surprise tactics, Shula had not informed us what the programme for the afternoon would be or who the audience would consist of. We expected to speak to a group of social workers. On arrival, we discovered that we were the sole presenters, and the list of attendees included our National Director of Mind, Judy Clements, and others whose names I had, until then, only seen on the covers of books. To say this created an instant nervous reaction would be an understatement. However, there were some familiar, friendly faces in the audience such as Jan Wallcraft. Professor Peter Beresford introduced us, and the audience were most receptive and excited about our endeavours. Karen and Linda spoke and answered questions with a new kind of insight for researchers. Experiencing a sense of achievement, we were quite 'high' during the train journey home.

Three local talks were to follow in the first half of the year. We were assisted in these presentations by Neil Coxhead, a local consultant psychiatrist who had taken a particular interest in our study. Dr Coxhead spoke of the 'unholy alliance' which had evolved between psychiatry and psychoanalysis. Freud had interpreted the early abusive experiences of his patients as a kind of hysteria, which constituted false memory syndrome. Concurrently, biological psychiatry had tended to marginalise post traumatic symptomatology, resulting in a lack of legitimacy regarding mental illness classification and access to treatment. He pointed out that this 'alliance' had set back the course of history in relation to effective responses for those who have attracted a diagnosis of Personality Disorder. Four service users were involved in these local presentations, Karen, Linda, Lesley and Kathy. Reading user quotes from the research, they spoke with great feeling and presented these perspectives in a very moving way. The first talk was given to a large number of local professionals and was probably much too long. However, we expected a lively response and lots of questions. At the conclusion of our presentation we were greeted by a stunned silence. Perhaps it was all too close to home, this relating of some of the terrible experiences of service users from the local area. Like the tale of 'The Emperor's New Clothes', local service users were pointing to a stark truth. Our second presentation was to the medical group and included many local psychiatrists. This encompassed more debate at question time, although some seemed to prefer more of a discussion as we were packing up to leave. This was quite good fun because there is nothing that Lesley likes more than a good argument with a psychiatrist. The third talk took place at the local acute hospital. Interestingly, almost all service users involved were unwilling to take part in a presentation that might include, in the audience, nurses who had been involved in their care. Lesley, now living out of the area, travelled from Northamptonshire to help with the talk.

One of our most important conferences, 'Public Protection', was held in October 2000. We were asked to share a platform with Mike Boyle, the head of the Home Office Mental Health Division, who now cited some 2500 people as likely candidates for preventative detention. Representatives from the prison service and Special Hospitals spoke of the new assessment and treatment pilots at Whitemore Prison and Rampton Hospital. We were pleased to hear Dr Pete Snowden, former Chair of the Forensic Faculty of the Royal College of Psychiatrists, say from the stage that he believed his colleagues, including forensic psychiatrists, had a poor grasp on the meaning of this category. Dr Phil Fennel spoke on law and was our master of ceremonies for the day. His insight regarding mental health law is something I had long admired. He introduced our talk and we had 20 minutes to make it really count. So scary had been the prospect of this conference that only Linda had been willing to accompany me. We picked out relevant themes from our research. Linda had been responsible for interviewing most of the forensic component of our sample whom she affectionately nicknamed 'the naughty boys'. Becoming increasingly distressed by the 'objective' exposition of people's lives during the course of the conference, she sat on the stage crying, and pinched her arm and said, 'I'm real, please treat me like a human being'. Dr Todd Hogue, from Rampton, observed that there had been much said about the people in this category and now here was the service user coming back to us again in this forum. After our presentation we nipped out for a cigarette with Phil Fennel. We were not allowed even to smoke on the steps because, after all, the venue was the Royal College of Surgeons. We were relegated to the roadside and, while we smoked, Linda gave an impromptu interview to the press on the pavement. Phil said he thought our talk was great. However, we felt we had received a mixed reception. The consensus of the day seemed to be to move forward regarding plans for the inclusion of preventative detention in a new Mental Health Act, and to take stock of the assessment and treatment pilots. I was particularly pleased to meet one kindred spirit from the audience, Sue Johnson, co-founder of the James Naylor Foundation. Sue gave me a lilac-coloured leaflet about their organisation which appeared to espouse most of our dearly held beliefs.

Other conferences were to include 'Mad, Bad or just misunderstood?', held at Regents College in London. Here leading figures in the field, Dr Gwen Adshed from Boadmoor and Professor Connar Duggan, spoke of Personality Disorder being a poor measure. Lesley and Karen helped to present our results. Valerie Sinasson, Director of the Clinic for Dissociative Studies, gave a paper entitled 'Personality Disorder, a rude word for trauma', which was very well received, especially by Lesley. 'In her presentation Valerie put the "person" back into Personality Disorder. She spoke of how childhood experiences affect our very being and, although I found some of her case information somewhat harrowing, it was portrayed in the right context, with great understanding, and was not gratuitous.' We heard more about some of the enlightening work being carried out at Grendon Underwood Therapeutic Prison, and Dr Rex Haigh, from the Winterbourne Centre, explained how therapeutic communities can be a very effective day service.

Just a few weeks later, at the end of March 2001, a most interesting conference was convened by Bob and Sue Johnson of the James Naylor Foundation and held at the Friends House in Euston Road, London. We soon realised that this was a different kind of conference. The audience was large, some three to four hundred people, consisting of Quakers, mental health professionals, and service users from Borderline UK and many areas of the country. Julian and Mary Ann had accompanied me to help with our presentation and we began to realise that, for the first time, our talk would not be the only one given by service users. No fewer than five service users would speak from the platform that day. The most moving speaker was a prisoner from Grendon Underwood Prison. Many of us were moved to tears. Mary Ann sat next to me and cried.

> I thought the Conference was amazing and I got a lot out of it. It wasn't exactly enjoyment because it was a serious and emotional day. It was very powerful and it made me frustrated because I had a lot to say. But I got up on that stage and I said some of it – I strutted my stuff! The prisoner from Grendon Therapeutic Prison was the most moving. What he said made me cry. I had strong feelings about listening to a sex offender. I felt he was very brave to confront several hundred people at the risk of being ostracised. I went up afterwards to reassure him and to thank him for helping me to understand.

Our friend from Grendon had this to say about the day:

> What I found so amazing was all these people who just wanted to say to
> me 'thank you, you have helped me'. That meant so much and has given
> me a lot of strength to face my own fears and anxieties concerning the
> future. It is important for me as a person labelled with Personality
> Disorder, which has arisen as a consequence of traumatic childhood expe-
> riences, that I am understood rather than just being contained and con-
> trolled. In understanding my own abuse, the trauma and pain associated
> with the above, I am able to understand the trauma, pain and experiences
> that I put my own victims through. I would like to give back to the outside
> community – to help heal the wounds, the trauma and pain others have
> experienced through abuse. This is why I want to help your Foundation.
> After the morning session, this young lady approached me and thanked
> me for helping her to understand her own abuse and her hatred towards
> people like myself. She told me that I had helped her to see that, even
> though I'm a sex offender, I too have suffered and that she could
> empathise with me and that removed the hatred. This young lady gave me
> a lot of support and encouragement for which I would like to thank her.

To date, the results of the research have been presented 18 times at local,
regional and national venues. Yet another instructive attendance was for the
South London and Maudsley NHS Trust. Here, Felicity de Zueleta was in the
audience to see that we had spelt her name incorrectly on one of our overheads.
It was on this occasion that we heard Dr Ian Kerr, who had worked closely for
some years with the man who developed Cognitive Analytic Therapy, Anthony
Ryle. Dr Kerr spoke about the idea of 'the ailment as ignorance', that is, that a
lack of understanding may cause others to regard an individual as a difficult
patient and this further affects that person's mental health in an adverse way. He
explained that behaviour is also a form of communication and that the way in
which a system responds to this behaviour may also be dysfunctional. He urged
us to see things in a 'systemic' way as a series of dynamics being enacted around
that person. Services and people around the client may be reacting in a variety
of ways, identifying and sympathising with them, getting angry with and
rejecting them, feeling guilty or burnt out – a variety of responses which fall
short of actually understanding how it is for that individual. CAT maps out this
whole system which exists around the person in a very practical and understandable way. The map may be used just as a tool for professionals to help them
better understand; however, it can be used directly with the client. There is
room for everyone on the map, parents, partner, even the receptionist you might

have had bother with last week, even the Home Office if you are worried about Mental Health Act proposals. This systemic conceptual framework, which can be a powerful tool for self-reflection, was described in the words of one of Dr Kerr's patients: 'All my life I felt like a disconnected group of islands – now I have a map of it.'

The conference experience not only increased our confidence and enabled us to disseminate our findings, it was also a wonderful opportunity to meet all those listed above and many others such as Chris Scanlon, Principal Psychotherapist from the Henderson Hospital. He expressed some enthusiasm for our research and pointed out that the Henderson itself was founded on the principle of unresolved trauma, being originally set up in 1947 to treat psychological casualties from the Second World War. We met Pip Bevan of the National Homeless Alliance. Pip is a priest who has worked with the homeless for many years. He stressed that this is not a new client group, but rather one that has been recently recognised. Additionally, Professor Louis Appleby had become the National Director for Mental Health. During this time he made a visit to North Essex. Our Director of Mental Health at the local Health Authority, Mike O'Keeffe, suggested that he might like to read a copy of our research report. I gave a copy to Professor Appleby and he wrote to us saying how much he had enjoyed reading it on the train journey home, and that he was glad to see we had referenced his old research paper 'The patients psychiatrists dislike'.

We also began to spread the word in a number of publications. An early paper, and one of our most exciting publications, was printed in October 2000 in *Mental Health Care* magazine (Castillo 2000). We discovered that the editor, Catherine Jackson, had accorded us no less than nine pages of the magazine, including a 'moody shot' front cover photograph. This aptly showed four of us posing in black against a backdrop of black. I remember well running through the acute hospital, upstairs and downstairs, clutching a copy of the journal and showing it to as many people as I could find. Some articles were co-written with service users involved in the research. One was co-authored with Dr Coxhead and entitled 'The hurtfulness of a diagnosis'. We submitted this to the magazine of the Royal College of Psychiatrists, the *Psychiatric Bulletin*, in an effort to gain publication in a clinical rather than a discursive journal. However, with great disappointment we received our only rejection to date. Not to be discouraged, we submitted the exact same article to the journal of the Royal College of Nursing, *Mental Health Practice*, and it was published in June 2001 (Castillo, Allen and Coxhead 2001). Our eighth publication was co-authored with Professor Ramon and Dr Morant. It appeared as the lead article in the

2001 winter edition of the *International Journal of Social Psychiatry* (Ramon, Castillo and Morant 2001). I guessed it had been published before we received the copy because we began to receive phone calls from doctors. We had become international.

CHAPTER 16

New Beginnings

If the angel deigns to come it will be because you have convinced her, not by tears but by your humble resolve to be always beginning: to be a beginner.

Rainer Maria Rilke (1926, p.97)

Significantly, our research report was completed in February 2000, at the beginning of a new millennium. I had fulfilled my role as 'midwife' and had acted as a witness to this emerging account of the inner world of those who had attracted a diagnosis of Personality Disorder. I imagine that some of you are asking what has become of the service users involved in this study and to what degree our endeavors have had an impact. The archetype of co-operation is a partnership between equals for the purpose of growth. My first partner in this journey was Lesley Allen, whose letter to the Health Authority in 1997 might be seen as the 'prime mover' in this story. Lesley continues to be an invaluable partner in this work and has expressed the following thoughts:

> This experience has indeed been emancipating. It has given us a voice and an opportunity to put forward our side of the story and tell you how it really feels. This is an opportunity we have made the most of. Often with shaky legs and trembling voices, we have spoken our truth on platforms shared with some of the most famous names in the field. For once in our traumatic lives we have felt valued and respected. Slowly we are seeing a shift in the views of some professionals who no longer see Personality Disorder as untreatable and are helping to develop excellent long term programmes which are increasingly proving that this is not the case.

Of our four user researchers, Karen has now been discharged from mental health services altogether. She has expressed great gratitude to her care co-ordinator of many years and to the therapist who has worked with her so effectively over the past two years. 'When I look back at all the years of struggle, and even how bad I was 18 months ago, I want to say one thing to you, DON'T

GIVE UP. It is possible to get better and I really do have a life now.' The indomitable Linda says, 'Well, I still have my children, they will never manage to take them away from me'. Julian is preparing to resume his degree which was interrupted by mental illness so many years ago, in Australia. Raine works as a mental health advocate in a hospital in another town. They live on with insight but not totally unburdened of illness. Others involved in the research have moved on, got married, managed to get their children back, have started academic courses and have even begun part-time work. However, others still struggle. For this reason we re-formed our group at the beginning of 2001. Current members of the Personality Disorder support group are usually experiencing great difficulties. Access to meaningful support and services is frequently the focus of the afternoon. One member left us recently to begin Dialectical Behaviour Therapy, one is now resident at the Henderson Hospital, and another had this to say about the group:

> The surroundings are the warm innards of a converted church, now home to the North Gate Centre. Allocated a room at the front of the building, the Personality Disorder Group meets in Colchester for the purposes of mutual support and friendship. Everyone who has had a diagnosis of Personality Disorder, or who adheres to some or all of the vague symptoms of one of the many Personality Disorder categories, is welcome. We sit around supping tea/coffee, munching biscuits and taking it in turn to talk and share. The group is greatly accepting which allows members to 'open their hearts' and share deeply moving stories in safety. It is not just being able to feel solace in hearing someone who has the same feelings as your own, but people are able to offer advice and coping mechanisms that have worked for them in the past. This is an opportunity not just for airing thoughts but an arena for discussion. I joined the group three months ago fresh out of a spell in hospital. I have found the group a haven of like minds each struggling with their own personal demons but willing to take some time out and offer their extensive experience to help others. I myself gain greatly from offering past and present coping strategies to the group in the hope that they will aid in helping someone over their hurdles. Although I find it difficult to share, I have found the ease of others' talk has loosened the tight strings I hold on my emotions and I have been able to add to the discussion, something I felt unable to do even on an individual basis with many people. I believe that for me the need for acceptance, commonly hard to find amongst the services for people with the Personality Disorder diagnosis, has been met in part by this group. (Anonymous 2001b)

Early in 2001 Lesley and I also began to publish a monthly news-sheet entitled *Personality Disorder North Essex News*, which now has a national circulation. Both service users and professionals contribute articles and make up the distribution list. With our now-accustomed boldness, we even send an unsolicited copy to the Home Office each month. A regular feature of the news-sheet is 'Service Users Speak'. Here local service users continue to explore issues concerning their condition and treatment, and the following article gives some measure of the evolvement of services in this area.

> I can't imagine what it is like for nurses to look after people like me who have this kind of condition. It takes dedication and an awful lot of patience. I feel Colchester has moved forward in that the services are now willing to accept this kind of burden. Ultimately it isn't exactly what we need, and patient and nurse become trapped in a kind of endless cycle. But, until the system has evolved new and better ways to respond to those of us who are so traumatised that our self-destructiveness seems bottomless, how else do we cope unless we have your care and support? So, the services in this area have taken a huge step forward in making a place for us. The standard of nursing I have encountered during this admission has been out of this world. And my consultant has been patient, responsive, flexible and just wonderful. I am only annoyed that she won't take me home to live with her, but I'm working on it! (Warner 2002)

However, criminal justice matters remain fraught with difficulties. One service user writes as follows about her experiences:

> I have always said I wanted someone to take control of my life, but every time someone tries I go berserk. I wanted a book…and still do…a page-by-page book on what to do, where to go, how to think. When I look back at the 15-year struggle I see the same ten-year-old child fighting the system she couldn't win. The same fears of being locked up but, in a bizarre way, feeling that is what I want. Finally, last year I was driven to my limits and took my anger and frustration out on a man who worked inside The League of Friends shop. I was on Section and, for the hundredth time, I was on 'one to one' but finally escaped and with a piece of crockery held up to the man's neck demanded £10. I didn't need the money nor did I intend to hurt the man, but suddenly I was no longer in the mental health system but the judicial system. Thirty-five secure units turned me away and I finally ended up in the psychiatric unit at Holloway prison. Another revolving door syndrome! Inmates couldn't hack the outside world but preferred the rigid routine of prison. I must admit I became a model

prisoner, only self-harming three times in five months. At the end of the five months I was sent to a low secure hospital and again started to regress to the ten-year-old child. 'Please,' I begged, 'give me something to do, I'll paint the walls' – anything to relieve the boredom of being locked in an eight-bedroomed wing. You see, even though I didn't like prison I was always given the jobs of cleaning the staff office, staff loos, serving the food. I felt I was trusted and well liked. In hospital, I finally became like an animal, not only self-harming but smashing the place up, and for six months I was on 'one to one'. They labelled me a 'psychopath' and I joked about being Norman Bates's sister, but inside I was hurt and afraid. After six months I was released and returned to the community to heal my wounds, except I couldn't make such a big change and took to my bed for four months, too afraid to go out of my room in case I might hurt someone. After all I was a 'PSYCHOPATH' – someone with no con-science. (Anonymous 2001c)

Family members also have something very meaningful to say in relation to recidivism as illustrated by this sisters' story.

It is now the fifth Christmas that my brother will have spent in one prison or another. He came to our family when he was three-and-a-half years old. His early life was very chaotic. His mother was a heroin addict and also had a diagnosis of paranoid schizophrenia. The police were frequently called because he was left alone so often as a baby. He was very malnourished and was born addicted. He was fed so much sugar that, when he came to us, he looked like a third-world victim of malnutrition, with a little pot belly. I was seven when he came to us, and he was very afraid of being left on his own and had been told that he wasn't wanted by anyone. I believe there were also signs of sexual abuse. I am absolutely convinced that these early issues shaped his life. The person is formed at a very early age. He came to a very loving family and he was, and still is, adored by us. But this wasn't enough. To see him every day is to see him live in torment. The pain behind his eyes is almost too much to bear. He was scapegoated at school for his racial differences and there was truancy from every school he went to. He was a very intelligent child and they didn't know how to deal with him. They saw him as bad. Then his mother died and he disappeared for a year. He was sleeping rough, and at the age of 14 he was raped. When we found him he looked like a caged animal. He's been in secure units for over half his life now, in and out of psychiatric hospital and prison. When he is released he is put in B&Bs where they are dealing drugs, or the night shelter. I believe that being in the outside world is terrifying for him. He gets so frightened that he tries to access hospital or he re-offends because he knows it's an easy way to get back to somewhere where he has food, shelter and relative peace. It is also a way to obtain easy access to drugs on the prison wing. I do try to be positive about the future but it's hard to see a solution. What I would hope for is a chance of supported housing and an opportunity to do some sheltered work to try to help him gain some self-esteem. I would like him to feel at peace with himself and to know that he would receive some real help from mental health services. That they won't just see him as bad and a drug user. He is ill, he is not well. He needs to be helped to feel that he is legitimate and to know that he matters. (Anonymous 2002)

One mother expresses grave concerns over the recent fate of her daughter.

When she was first diagnosed 12 years ago, the psychiatrist told us that our daughter had paranoid schizophrenia. He said that normally his patients had five out of ten possible symptoms but that she had nine out of ten. Now I am told by her current psychiatrist that she doesn't have schizophrenia but personality problems. He says that if I bring her back in a couple of years, when there is a new Mental Health Act, then he will be able to lock her up. At the time she was admitted to hospital she was evicted from her home and had also assaulted someone. Now she has been kicked out with nothing, no home, no money, no medication, no aftercare, and the police are looking for her to interview her about the assault. You walk into a room after 12 years of hell to be told she's not ill. What have they been doing for 12 years? I want some answers. (Anonymous 2002)

In July 1999 the Department of Health and the Home Office issued their policy proposals for managing people considered to have Dangerous Severe Personality Disorder. Here the intention was first stated that those so diagnosed should be segregated in specialist treatment units potentially without limit of time. In December 2000 proposals for a new Mental Health Act were outlined in the White Paper 'Reforming the Mental Health Act' (DoH 2000). On 25 June 2002, the draft Mental Health Bill (DoH 2002) was submitted to Parliament. The preceding White Paper set out government proposals for Dangerous Severe Personality Disorder in a separate section. However, whether out of an effort to skilfully sidestep the diagnostic confusions surrounding the label, or possibly suspecting that not many people outside government accept Dangerous Severe Personality Disorder as a meaningful diagnosis, the term has been left out of the proposed Act. The word 'psychopathic' has also been removed from the Act and the language is generally more respectful.

Mental disorder is defined in the Act as 'any disability or disorder of mind or brain which results in an impairment or disturbance of mental functioning'. Second, the mental disorder must be 'of such a nature or degree as to warrant provision of medical treatment', and third, 'in the case of a patient who is at substantial risk of causing serious harm to other persons, that it is necessary for the protection of those persons that medical treatment be provided.' Although terminology lacks transparency, it is not difficult to deduce that the new definition of mental disorder is designed to close the legal loophole regarding the treatability clause in the current Act because this has made it difficult to remove from society those considered to be dangerously disturbed unless they have committed a crime.

There is no doubt that these proposals are disaster driven and particularly impelled by the murder of Lin Russell and her six-year-old daughter by Michael Stone in 1996. After such events and their media coverage, the consensus of public opinion may be that dangerous people should not be allowed to walk around freely. But how do we know who they are? Even Shaun Russell, the husband and father of Michael Stone's victims, has expressed doubts. 'I would be very keen to see these measures trialled and tested so that there is minimal chance of people being wrongly detained' (Moller 2002). Dr Tony Zigmond, Chairman of the Royal College of Psychiatrists' General Adult Faculty, is concerned that working out who should be detained could be extremely difficult. 'Predicting dangerousness is an imprecise art.' (Moller 2002) He considers that this could mean the detention of up to 5000 people who haven't done anything wrong. Health Minister Jacqui Smith considers that there are between 2100 and 2400 people in the UK with Severe Personality Disorder but that the vast majority are in prison or secure mental hospital, leaving 300 to 600 in the community. She has stated that 36 extra hospital places have been created at Whitemore Prison in Cambridgeshire and that there are plans to create a further 200 places at Broadmoor and Rampton Special Hospitals (Carvel and Ward 2002). In addition to concern over the government's theoretical notions regarding sufferers and the degree of service provision needed, worrying statements continue to appear in the press concerning the fact that Dangerous Severe Personality Disorder is not considered to be treatable, yet proposals include detention for the purpose of treatment (Johnson 2002). Additional mathematical anomalies include the government's assessment of the need for 100 extra psychiatrists to sit as medical members on Appeal Tribunals for those who wish to challenge their detention. The Royal

College of Psychiatrists considers that the new Act would collapse under the weight of its own regulatory framework because, they estimate, a further 600 psychiatrists would be needed for the Mental Health Review Tribunal system alone, and it would be impossible to recruit such numbers.

Although the draft Mental Health Bill required a 12-week consultation period, within days of its being made public the Royal College, together with the Law Society, issued a joint statement condemning proposed reforms on grounds of inadequate resources and distorted rationale. Focusing in part on the issue of Dangerous Severe Personality Disorder, the statement highlights the fact that such widening of criteria for detention would mean that large numbers would find themselves inappropriately detained. John Cox, President of the Royal College of Psychiatrists, stated, 'Why is the government proposing to spend millions of pounds on legislation that we all oppose when it should be putting it into services for patients?' (Moller 2002)

Encompassed within the difficult question of balancing public protection with individual civil liberties, one might ask why people who need help now aren't getting it. In addition to resource issues the dilemma of treatability disputes must be acknowledged. Here the experiences of our local service users may give clues to intrinsic flaws within government plans. Recently the findings of yet another public inquiry were published in our area (North Essex Health Authority 2002). Within its pages one can read how a patient in an acute hospital presented as untreatable because of dual diagnosis of substance misuse problems. He was assessed for transfer to both low and medium secure hospitals and refused. Subsequently discharged to the community, he murdered his mother. Today some service users with long mental health, and seriously assaultative, histories continue to receive such a response. One client recently supported by our advocacy service stated a strong wish to be transferred to secure hospital, yet he was rejected as not mentally ill on grounds of untreatability, then discharged from acute in-patient care to the community. One of our greatest concerns is that traumatised or misdiagnosed service users will offend and continue to find their way into the criminal justice system, as described below by one service user who took part in the study.

> I was in hospital for a bi-polar condition. My diagnosis was changed by a locum psychiatrist. Within a few days I was discharged without money/ benefits, medication or proper aftercare, into inadequate accommodation – with so-called 'untreatable Personality Disorder'. I fell into the hands of the police as I was wandering around Colchester aimlessly, and for two consecutive nights I was held in a police cell because I was so ill. The con-

sultant would not readmit me, either informally or under section. I was taken to court on a harassment charge, in a prison van, in handcuffs, held in the cells beneath the magistrates' court. I would have been sent to the remand centre at Holloway Prison, if I had not been collected by my parents and sent back on bail to Wales. We made a difficult and dangerous journey in my parents' car. During a break in the journey I was described by a doctor as practically 'psychotic' and 'very manic'. He advised my parents to get me into hospital as soon as possible. When we arrived home I was sectioned and treated as bi-polar, *not* Personality Disordered. Once again, with the right medication and adequate therapeutic support, I gradually became very well again.

One might argue that such a new Mental Health Act as is being proposed might broker a better deal for service users like those described above. However, under such an Act, would a new kind of 'disliked-patient syndrome' emerge? Today it may be decided that someone is not mentally ill but rather Personality Disordered and untreatable. Tomorrow it may be that they are considered not to be Personality Disordered but simply a criminal.

Concerns which remain in relation to Mental Health Act proposals include whether this is a law which discriminates against those foolish enough to disclose their thoughts, and will people who need help be driven underground? And what of treatability for those who are considered dangerous, but not the most dangerous, who might become detained under such an Act? To treat this condition one has to understand it. Therefore, would they become subjected merely to a containment regime with insufficient understanding and inadequate therapeutic interventions? The underpinning ideologies of many units throughout the country which may be used for this purpose require radical rethinking, but will sufficient investment for this be forthcoming? This is a law that affects a whole nation, and, if such a transformation in treatment regimes does not occur widely, any kind of proposals for preventative detention are morally flawed. 'The Mental Health Bill may be a crowd-pleaser, but it will not help as much as well-directed funding' (Moller 2002).

Local service users continue to campaign *for* preventative treatment strategies, and *against* preventative detention. Such aspirations include the more comprehensive availability of psychotherapeutic treatments such as CAT and DBT, the provision of a day service run as a therapeutic community, and the opening of a local safe centre and crisis house. A crisis house pilot is now being planned for Colchester and our group has become part of the consultation process.

Early in 2002, I was contacted by Alison Hooper, Senior Policy Manager for Mental Health at the Department of Health. Alison explained that a group had been formed to create a 'National Personality Disorder Strategy'. She was interested in our study and how the group might meaningfully incorporate the views of service users within the strategy. On 19 March I was invited to attend a strategy group meeting at the Department of Health where Anthony Bateman, Peter Tyrer, Tom Fahey and others sat around the table and listened to my account of the work on Personality Disorder service users had carried out in North East Essex. The strategy group decided to hold a series of focus groups, to be facilitated by Rex Haigh of the Winterbourne Therapeutic Community Day Centre. It was planned that these groups would involve service users with a Personality Disorder diagnosis from different parts of the country, and would look at Personality Disorder services in general adult mental health. Other parts of the strategy include forensic services and staff training. The service user focus groups are now underway and involve representatives from our area. Cameron, Mary Ann and Lesley report as follows.

> One of my contributions was to point out that, *it's a very sticky label*, once you have it, it's very difficult to get rid of it. I also spoke about the lack of outreach services to help someone to bridge after attending somewhere specialist like the Henderson Hospital. Local services are beginning to be proposed. For example, a crisis house and safe centre are being planned for Colchester. We need this service very much. I spoke about re-education of the public and about stigma, stereotypical attitudes stemming from sensational events such as the Michael Stone case. I and others also spoke of the need to tackle Personality Disorder at a much earlier age. I was pleased to hear about someone else at the focus group who had really benefited from DBT, because I hope to start that soon – I'm on the waiting list.

> I found it encouraging because the way the Department of Health was coming across made me feel as if they really want to do something. I felt that the lack of services and of appropriate support was really highlighted. You can experience decades of abuse and are expected to get better in a few months, whereas sometimes years of treatment are needed. People ask for help, and they ask and ask. Eventually something drastic happens and it's too late – suicide or murder.

> We were informed that all Mental Health Trusts were asked to complete a questionnaire detailing the services that they currently provide, and 90 per cent of Trusts had replied. Of those Mental Health Trusts that did reply,

one-third said that they made no provision for those with a Personality Disorder. A further third of Trusts said that they provided limited services, leaving the remainder that did make provision. Rex Haigh took us through the five services that are currently available for those with a Personality Disorder, giving a brief insight into what each one consists of. The five are, Cognitive Behavioural Therapy, CBT, Dialectical Behavioural Therapy, DBT, Cognitive Analytic Therapy, CAT, Psychoanalysis in a day hospital, and Therapeutic Communities.

Within this meaningful dialogue, concerns about sufficient investment remain. The possibility of therapeutic community day services has been mentioned…one for each Trust. However, in, for example, a wide Trust area like North Essex, a facility such as this would only be of benefit to service users in the town in which it is sited. The Department of Health is eliciting relevant views from the 'horse's mouth', and with very little coaxing. But service users remain cautious about the implementation of their views. With proposed investment into specialist services for supposed Dangerous Severe Personality Disorder estimated at over 120 million pounds, they wonder what will be left for local mental health services and preventative work with young people (Oats 2002). We proceed with hope, and a sense of achievement about how far we have come, in that the discourse is now with the national policy makers. However, it is with cautious optimism that we take our place in this new climate of user-centred services because this essential consultation is occurring against a background of proposed, potentially costly and repressive legislation, which fundamentally misses the point.

As far as we are aware, this is the first full-scale research study which has involved service users in directly researching clinical and diagnostic issues. We believe our study demonstrates that a group of service users can produce something new and fruitful in the field of mental health research. Service users have shown that those who are still in the midst of their difficulties can, with support, effectively and powerfully define themselves within a system and so contribute to scientific knowledge. Their proposed construct points overwhelmingly to a need for a more humane response and a redefining of this diagnosis into a category which more clearly suggests aetiology and offers a better understanding of this human condition.

References

Acland, J. (1997) 'Care of Clients with Personality Disorder.' Letter from Acute Strategy Group, North Essex Mental Health Trust to North Essex Health Authority.

Acland, J. (1999) *Damaged Personality Formulation.* Colchester: North Essex Mental Health Partnership NHS Trust.

Ainscough, C. and Toon, K. (1996) *Breaking Free: Help for Survivors of Child Sexual Abuse.* London: Sheldon Press.

Aldgate, J. and Tunstill, J. (1995) *Making Sense of Section 17: Implementing Services for Children in Need within the 1989 Children Act.* London: HMSO.

Allen, L. (1997) Letter to North Essex Health Authority published in *Linking Hands: North Essex Service User Journal 8.*

Allen, L, (2002) 'Report from the second Department of Health focus groups.' *Personality Disorder: North Essex News 14,* 2.

Anonymous (2001a) 'On the receiving end.' *Human Givens: Radical Psychology Today 8,* 2, 17–21.

Anonymous (2001b) 'Personality Disorder support group.' *Personality Disorder: North Essex News 10,* 2.

Anonymous (2001c) 'My Story.' *Personality Disorder: North Essex News 8,* 2.

Anonymous (2002) Untitled. *Personality Disorder: North Essex News 11,* 3.

Bateman, A. (1997) 'Borderline Personality Disorder and psychotherapeutic psychiatry: An integrated approach.' *British Journal of Psychotherapy 13,* 4, 489–498.

Beeforth, M., Conlan, E. and Grayley, R. (1994) *Have We Got Views for You.* London: The Sainsbury Centre.

Bell, E. and McCann, R. (1996) 'Borderline Personality Disorder'. In S. Jackobson (ed) *Psychiatric Secrets.* Philadelphia: Belfrens Medical Publishers.

Bender, L. and Yarnell, H. (1941) 'An observation nursery.' *Journal of Social Psychiatry 97,* 1158–1174.

Bowlby, J. (1988) *A Secure Base.* London: Routledge.

Bracken, P. and Thomas, P. (1998) 'Post psychiatry: Broken promises and fractured dreams.' *Open Mind 88,* 18; 'A new debate in mental health.' *Open Mind 89,* 17; 'Mental health legislation: Time for a real change.' *Open Mind 90,* 17.

Bracken, P. and Thomas, P. (2000) 'Post modern diagnosis.' *Open Mind 106,*10.

Bradshaw, J. (1993) *Creating Love – The Next Great Stage of Growth.* London: Piatkus.

Brandon, D. (1991) *Innovation Without Change? Consumer Power in Psychiatric Services.* London: Macmillan.

Britton, P. (1998) *The Jigsaw Man.* London: Corgi.

Brown, G. and Harris, T. (1978) *Social Origins of Depression.* London: Unwin and Hyman.

Brown, G. and Harris, T. (1989) *Life Events and Illness.* London: Unwin and Hyman.

Burlingham, D. and Freud, A. (1942) *Young Children in War-Time London.* London: Allen and Unwin.

Carvel, J. and Ward, L. (2002) 'Detention plan for "dangerous" mental patients.' *Guardian,* 26 June.

Castillo, H. (2000) 'Users' views on the nature and treatment of Personality Disorder.' *Mental Health Care 4*, 2, 53–58.

Castillo, H., Allen, L. and Coxhead, N. (2001) 'The hurtfulness of a diagnosis.' *Mental Health Practice 4*, 9, 16–19.

Christiansen, K. (1970) 'Crime in the Danish twin population.' *Acta Geneticae Medicae et Gemellogiae 19*, 323–326.

Clark, L. and Livesley, W. (1996) 'Converging of two systems for assessing Personality Disorder.' *Psychological Assessment 8*, 294–303.

Cleckly, H. (1941) *The Mask of Sanity.* St. Louis: C.V. Mosby.

Clift, I. (1999) 'Personality Disorder: Time for a new approach.' *Mental Health Practice 2*, 10, 35–38.

Coid, J. (1989) 'Psychopathic disorders.' *Current Opinion in Psychiatry 2*, 750–756.

Coulter, J. (1973) *Approaches to Insanity.* Basingstoke: Robertson.

DoH (Department of Health) (1989) *The Care of Children: Principles and Practice in Guidance and Regulations.* London: HMSO.

DoH (Department of Health) (1991) *Patterns and Outcomes in Child Placement: Messages from Current Research and their Implications.* London: HMSO.

DoH (Department of Health) (1995) *Building Bridges: A Guide to Arrangements for Inter-Agency Working for the Care and Protection of Severely Mentally Ill People.* London: HMSO.

DoH (Department of Health) (1998) *Our Healthier Nation: A Contract for Health.* London: HMSO.

DoH (Department of Health) (1999a) *Managing Dangerous People with Severe Personality Disorder.* London: HMSO.

DoH (Department of Health) (1999b) *The National Service Framework for Mental Health.* London: HMSO.

DoH (Department of Health) (2000) *Reforming the Mental Health Act.* London: HMSO.

DoH (Department of Health) (2002) *Draft Mental Health Bill.* London: HMSO.

DoH and SS (Department of Health and Social Security) (1985) *Social Work Decisions in Child Care, Recent Research Findings and their Implications.* London: HMSO.

Dolan, B., Norton, K. and Warren, F. (1996) 'Cost-offset following specialist treatment of severe Personality Disorder.' *Psychiatric Bulletin 30*, 1–5.

Dolan, B., Evans, C. and Wilson, J. (1992) 'Therapeutic community treatment for Personality Disordered adults – Change in neurotic symptomatology on follow up.' *The International Journal of Social Psychiatry 16*, 745–747.

Diggins, M. (2000) 'Innovation as a way of professional life.' In S. Ramon, (ed) *A Stakeholder's Approach to Innovation in Mental Health Services: A Reader for the 21st Century.* Brighton: Pavilion Publishing.

DSM 1 (1952) *Diagnostic and Statistical Manual of Mental Disorders 1st Edition.* Washington DC: American Psychiatric Association.

DSM III (1987) *Diagnostic and Statistical Manual of Mental Disorders (Revised).* Washington DC: American Psychiatric Association.

DSM IV (1994) *Diagnostic and Statistical Manual of Mental Disorders 4th Edition.* Washington DC: American Psychiatric Association.

Dunn, M. and Parry, G. (1997) 'A formulated care plan approach for people with Borderline Personality Disorder in a community health service setting.' *Clinical Psychology Forum 104*, 19–22.

Durkheim, E. (1970) *Suicide: A Study in Sociology.* London: Routledge and Kegal Paul.

Eastman, N. (1999) *Severe Personality Disorder – Who is Responsible?* Paper to National Conference, 16th June. London: Gateway.

Evans, C. and Fisher, M. (1999) 'Collaborative evaluation with service users. Moving towards user controlled research.' In I. Shaw, and J. Lishman, (eds) *Evaluation and Social Work Practice.* London: Sage.

Eysenck, H. (1975) *The Eysenck Personality Questionnaire.* London: University of London Press.

Fain, S. and Webster, P.F. (1953) 'Secret Love' from *Calamity Jane*, Warner Brothers.

Fenelon, F. (1997) *Playing for Time: Musicians of Auschwitz.* New York: Syracuse.

Fonagy, P. (1997) *When Cure is Inconceivable: The Aims of Psychoanalysis with Borderline Patients.* Paper to New York Freudian Society, 4 April.

Fonagy, P. (1999) 'The transmission of tansgenerational holocaust trauma.' *Attachment and Human Development 1,* 92–144.

Frankl, V. (1962) *Man's Search for Meaning.* London: Hodder and Stoughton.

Fransella, F. (1990) *Personal Construct Counselling in Action.* London: Sage.

Freire, P. (1970) *Pedagogy of the Oppressed.* New York: Herder and Herder.

Freud, S. (1909) *Analysis of a Phobia in a Five Year Old Boy.* London: Hogarth Press.

Gelder, M., Gath, D. and Mayou, R. (1989) 'Personality Disorder.' In *Oxford Text Book of Psychiatry 2nd Edition.* Oxford: Oxford Medical Publications.

Giles, T. (1985) 'Behavioural treatment of severe bulimia.' *Behaviour Therapy 16,* 393–405.

Gillan, A. and Campbell, D. (1998) Personality Disorder 'Untreatable'. *Guardian,* 24 October.

Glasgow, D. (1998) *Out of Sight, Out of Mind.* BBC, *Panorama,* 9 March.

Goffman, E. (1961) *Asylums: Essays on the Social Situation of Mental Patients and Other Inmates.* London: Penguin.

Goffman, E. (1963) *Stigma: Notes on the Management of Spoiled Identity.* London: Penguin.

Gostin, L. (1985) *Secure Provision.* London: Tavistock.

Guy, S. and Hume, A. (1999) 'A CBT strategy for offenders with Personality Disorders.' *Mental Health Practice 2,* 4,12–16.

Hare, R. (1991) *The Hare Psychopathy Checklist – Revised.* Toronto: Mental Health Care Systems.

Hargreaves, R. (1949) 'Consultation report to the United Nations.' In J. Bowlby *A Secure Base.* London: Routledge.

Henderson, D. (1939) *Psychopathic States.* New York: W.E. Norton.

Herman, J. (1992) 'Complex post traumatic stress disorder: A syndrome in survivors of prolonged and repeated trauma.' *Journal of Traumatic Stress Disorder 5,* 377–392.

Herman, J. and Van der Kolk, B. (1987) *Traumatic Origins of Borderline Personality Disorder in Psychological Trauma.* Washington DC: American Psychiatric Press.

Heron, J. (1981) 'Philosophical basis for a new paradigm.' In P. Reason, and J. Rowan, (eds) *Human Inquiry: A Sourcebook of New Paradigm Research.* Chichester: Wiley.

Hinshelwood, R. (1998) 'The difficult patient: The role of "scientific psychiatry" in understanding patients with chronic schizophrenia or severe Personality Disorder.' *British Journal of Psychotherapy,* Nov. 187–190.

Hunt, J. (1998) *Whistleblowing in the Social Services: Public Accountability and Professional Practice.* London: Arnold.

ICD 10 (1992) *Classification of Mental and Behavioural Disorders.* Geneva: World Health Organisation.

Johnson, R. (1999a) 'Predators.' *Panorama,* BBC.

Johnson, R. (1999b) 'Is Humanity Born Loveable, Sociable and Non-Violent?' Paper given at the Inaugural Conference of the James Naylor Foundation, 3–18, London, 24th April 1999.

Johnson, R. (2000) 'Defeating the Pessimism Surrounding Treatment'. Paper given at the Annual Conference of the James Naylor Foundation, 40–66, London, 29th April 2000.

Johnson, P. (2002) 'Dangerous patients face being locked up.' *Telegraph*, 26 June.

Jordan, C. and Ambrose, M. (2002) 'Influencing the national agenda.' *Personality Disorder: North Essex News 14*, 4.

Joseph, S., Yule, W. and Williams, R. (1997) *Understanding Post Traumatic Stress: A Psychological Perspective on Post Traumatic Stress Disorder and Treatment*. Chichester: Wiley.

Kelly, G. (1986) *A Brief Introduction to Personal Construct Theory*. London: Centre for Personal Construct Psychology.

Kernberg, O. (1984) *Severe Personality Disorders: Psychotherapeutic Strategies*. London: Yale University Press.

Kiehn, D. and Swales, M. (1995) 'An Overview of Dialectical Behaviour Therapy for the Treatment of Borderline Personality Disorder.' Mental Health Reading Room: Psychiatry On Line.

Klein, M. (1946) 'Some theoretical conclusions regarding the emotional life of the infant.' In P. Heimann, S. Isaaca and R. Riviere, *Developments in Psychoanalysis*. London: Hogarth.

Koch (1891) *Die Psychopathischen Minderwertigkeit*. [The Psychopathology of Inferiority.] Dorn: Ravensberg.

Kraepelin (1905) In M. Gelder, D. Gath and R. Mayou (eds) 'Personality Disorder'. In *Oxford Text Book of Psychiatry 2nd Edition*. Oxford: Oxford Medical Publications.

Kutchins, H. and Kirk, S. (eds) (1999) *Making us Crazy: DSM – The Psychiatric Bible and the Creation of Mental Disorders*. London: Constable.

Laing, R. (1971) *Knots*. London, New York: Penguin.

Laing, R. and Esterson, A. (1964) *Sanity, Madness and the Family*. London: Tavistock.

Lewis, G. and Appleby, L. (1988) 'Personality Disorder: The patients psychiatrists dislike.' *British Journal of Psychiatry 153*, 44–49.

Linehan, M. (1999) *Treating Borderline Personality Disorder*. London, New York: Guilford Press.

Linehan, M., Oldman, J. and Silk, K. (1995) 'Personality Disorder – Now what?' *Patient Care 29*,11, 75–79.

Main, M., Kaplan, W. and Cassidy, J. (1985) 'Security in infancy, childhood and adulthood.' In I. Bretherton, and E. Waters, (eds) *Growing Points of Attachment*. Society for Research in Child Development, Vol. 50.

Maudsley, H. (1884) In H. Kutchins, and S. A. Kirk, (eds) (1999) *Making us Crazy: DSM – The Psychiatric Bible and the Creation of Mental Disorders*. London: Constable.

Maudsley, H. (1885) In M. Gelder, D. Gath and R. Mayou (eds) 'Personality Disorder'. In *Oxford Text Book of Psychiatry 2nd Edition*. Oxford: Oxford Medical Publications.

Meichenbaum, D. (1994) *Treating Post Traumatic Stress Disorder: A Handbook and Practice Manual for Therapy*. Chichester: Wiley.

Menzies, D., Dolan, B. and Norton, K. (1993) 'Funding treatment for Personality Disorders: Are short term savings worth long term costs?' *Psychiatric Bulletin 7*, 517–519.

Merton, R. (1968) *Social Theory and Social Structure*. New York: The Free Press.

Moller, C. (2002) 'Mad, bad and dangerous.' *Guardian*, 27 June.

Morris, M. (1999) *Severe Personality Disorder: Who is Responsible?* Paper to National Conference, 16 June. London: Gateway.

Morrison, J. (1995) *DSM IV Made Easy*. London, New York: Ilford Press.

National Committee for Mental Hygiene (1918) *Statistical Manual for the Use of Institutions for the Insane*. New York: American Medico-Psychological Association.

Nemiah, J. (1995) 'Early concepts of trauma, dissociation and the unconscious: Their history and current implications.' In D. Bremner, and C. Marmar, (eds) *Trauma, Memory and Dissociation*. Washington DC: American Psychiatric Press.

North Essex Health Authority (1997) *Taking the Initiative Consultation Document: Rationing, Deciding Priorities and Service Restriction*. Public Health Directorate, Author.

North Essex Health Authority (2002) *Report of the Panel to Review the Care and Treatment Provided for Jonathan Neal*. Authors, North Essex Health Authority.

Norton, K. and Dolan, B. (1995) 'Acting out and the institutional response.' *The Journal of Forensic Psychiatry 6*, 2, 317–332.

Norton, K. and McGauley, G. (1998) *Counselling Difficult Clients*. London: Sage.

Norton, K. and Smith, S. (1994) *Problems with Patients: Managing Complicated Clinical Transactions*. Cambridge: Cambridge University Press.

Oats, P. (2002) 'Is there a need for a new label in mental health?' *Personality Disorder: North Essex News, Issue 14*, 2.

Oldham, J., Skodol, A., Kellman, H. (1992) 'Diagnosis by DSM III R Personality Disorders by two semi structured interviews – patterns of co-morbidity.' *American Journal of Psychiatry 149*, 213–220.

Oldham, J. (1994) 'Personality Disorders: Current perspectives.' *Journal of American Medical Association*, 272, 22, 1770–1779.

Oliver, M. (1992) 'Changing the social relations of research production.' *Disability, Handicap and Society 7*, 2, 101–114.

Ooi, R. (1997) Everyone's Life Has a Price. *Guardian*, 22 July.

Parks, P. (1990) *Rescuing the Inner Child: Therapy for Adults Sexually Abused as Children*. London: Souvenir Press.

Pilgrim, D. (1991) 'British Special Hospitals.' In S. Ramon, (ed) *British Special Hospitals in Psychiatry in Transition*. London: Pluto.

Pinel (1801) 'Personality Disorder.' In M. Gelder, D. Gath and R. Mayou (eds) (Ref. Kauka,1949, for translation) *Oxford Text Book of Psychiatry 2nd Edition*. Oxford: Oxford Medical Publications.

Pretzer, J. (1994) 'Cognitive therapy of Personality Disorders: The state of the art.' *American Journal of Clinical Psychology and Psychotherapy 1*, 5, 257–266.

Prins, H. (1995) *Offenders, Deviants or Patients?* London, New York: Routledge.

Pritchard (1835) In M. Gelder, D. Gath and R. Mayou (eds) 'Personality Disorder.' In *Oxford Text Book of Psychiatry 2nd Edition*. Oxford: Oxford Medical Publications.

Ramon, S. (1998) 'A scandalous category: Media representations of people suffering from mental illness.' In *Mental Illness in Europe*. London: MIND Publications.

Ramon, S. (2000) 'Participative mental health research: Users and professional researchers working together.' *Mental Health Care 3*, 7, 224–227.

Ramon, S., Castillo, H. and Morant, N. (2001) 'Experiencing Personality Disorder.' *International Journal of Social Psychiatry 47*, 4, 1–15.

Reber, A. (1985) *Dictionary of Psychology*. London, New York: Penguin.

Reed Report, The (1992) *Review of Health and Social Services for Mentally Disordered Offenders and Others Requiring Similar Services*. London: HMSO.

Reid vs Secretary of State for Scotland (1999) I ALL ER 481.

Rilke, R.M. (1926) *Letters: Pasternak, Tsvetayeva, Rilke*. Oxford: Oxford University Press.

Romme, M. and Escher, S. (1993) *Accepting Voices*. London: Mind Publications.

Rose, D., Ford, R., Linley, P. and Gawith, L. (1998) *In Our Experience: User Focused Monitoring of Mental Health Services in Kensington and Chelsea & Westminster Health Authority.* London: The Sainsbury Centre.

Roth, A. and Fonagy, P. (1997) *What Works for Whom?: A Critical Review of Psychotherapy Research.* London, New York: Guilford Press.

Rowe, D. (1997) 'Introduction.' In Kutchins, H. and Kirk, S. (eds) (1999) *Making us Crazy: DSM – The Psychiatric Bible and the Creation of Mental Disorders.* London: Constable.

Royal College of Psychiatrists (1999) *Offenders With Personality Disorder.* Council Report CR 71: Gaskell.

Royal College of Psychiatrists (2002) 'Reform of the Mental Health Act: Joint statement by the Royal College of Psychiatrists and the Law Society.' Press release, 27 June.

Rutter, M. (1987) 'Temperament, Personality and Personality Disorder.' *British Journal of Psychiatry 150,* 443–458.

Ryle, A. (1990) *Cognitive Analytic Therapy: Active Participation in Change.* Chichester: Wiley.

Ryle, A. (1997) *Cognitive Analytic Therapy: The Model and the Method.* Chichester: Wiley.

Schneider, K. (1923) *Psychopathic Personalities.* London: Cassell.

Schreiber, F. (1973) *Sybil.* Chicago: Henry Regnery.

Shorter, E. (1997) *A History of Psychiatry: From the Era of the Asylum to the Age of Prozac.* Chichester, New York: Wiley.

Stone, M. (1985) *Shellshock and the Psychologists – The Anatomy of Madness.* Volume 2. London: Tavistock.

Storey, L. and Dale, C. (1998) 'Meeting the needs of patients with severe Personality Disorders.' *Mental Health Practice 1,* 5, 20–26.

Szasz, T. (1961) *The Myth of Mental Illness.* London: Secker and Warburg.

Szasz, T. (1991) 'Diagnoses are not Diseases.' *The Lancet 338,* 1574–1576.

Tallis, D. (1997) 'A Criminal Waste of Life and Time.' *Guardian,* 5th February.

The Children Act (1989) London: HMSO.

The Lunacy Act (1890) London: HMSO.

The Mental Deficiency Act (1913) London: HMSO.

The Mental Health Act (1959) London: HMSO.

The Mental Health Act (1983) London: HMSO.

Turner, R. (1987) 'The effects of Personality Disorder diagnosis on the outcome of social anxiety symptom reduction.' *Journal of Personality Disorders 1,* 136–143.

Tyrer, P. (1988) *Personality Disorder, Management and Care.* London: Wright.

Tyrer, P. (2000) *Personality Disorders: Diagnosis, Management and Course.* Oxford: Butterworth Heinemann.

Tyrer, P. and Stein, H. (1993) *Studies of Outcome in Personality Disorder.* London: Wright.

Van der Kolk, B. (1996) *Traumatic Stress.* London and New York: Guilford Press.

Verrier, N. (1993) *The Primal Wound: Understanding the Adopted Child.* Baltimore: Gateway Press.

Warner, K. (2002) 'Am I for life?' *Personality Disorder: North Essex News 7,* 2.

Weinryb, R., Gustavasson, J. and Rossel, R., (1997) 'The Karolinska Psychodynamic Profile (KAPP): Studies of character and well-being.' *Psychoanalytic Psychology 14,* 495–515.

Whiteley, S. (1980) 'The Henderson Hospital – A community study.' *International Journal of Therapeutic Communities 1,* 1, 38–58.

Zueleta, F. de (1999) 'Borderline Personality as seen from an attachment perspective.' *Criminal Behaviour and Mental Health 9,* 237–253.

Subject Index

AA 92
abandonment 47, 59
abuse 64, 76–7, 125
  alcohol 47, 59, 77, 78
  counsellors 125
  cycle of 133
  drug 47, 59, 76, 77–8
  early emotional 47, 59, 61, 100, 110
  early sexual 47, 59, 61, 76, 99–101, 113, 143
  early violent 47, 59, 61
  later 47, 59
  survivors 112
accident and emergency (A & E) 81
  support from 48, 62
accommodation 95
acid indigestion 77
acting out 29
activities/occupation 87
adult convictions (prison) 47, 59
advocacy, as offering most help 91
advocate 74
  support from 48, 62, 63
affective disorders 13
age 45, 55
  and gender 56
agoraphobia 57, 58
AIDS 21
alcoholism 57, 58
alcohol misuse 47, 59, 77, 78, 112
alienation, urban 88
American Psychiatric Association 28, 135, 136
anankastic (ICD-10) 18
'Anger' 104
anger 47, 59, 65, 101, 104
  inability to express 75
Anglia Polytechnic University 7, 42, 147

anorexia 75
anti-depressants 92
antisocial (DSM-IV) 17
Antisocial Personality Disorder 15, 33, 136, 142, 144
anxiety 46, 57, 58, 75, 76, 77, 78, 142
anxious (avoidant) (ICD 10) 18
Appeal Tribunals 160
armed forces, support from 48, 62
Ashworth Special Hospital 35
attachment seeking behaviour 39, 66
Attachment Theory (Bowlby) 24, 66
Attention Deficit Hyperactivity Disorder 30
Auschwitz 33
avoidant (DSM-IV) 18
Axis 1 disorders 33

'badness' 70
bereavement 124
bingeing 77
Bi-polar Disorder 58
'Black Hole, The' (poem) 108
blaming self 76–7
Borderline Personality Disorder 15, 19, 31, 32, 33, 41, 46, 57, 59, 60, 61, 65, 142
  diagnosis (DSM-IV) 17
Borderline UK 151
bottled-up feelings 77
'Bouncing Back' (poem) 110
brain injury 57, 58
Bridge Project 132
Bristol Infirmary 13
Broadmoor Hospital 144, 151, 160
Building Bridges (DoH) 38
Bulger, Jamie 33
bulimia 76

care co-ordinator 90
Care Order 118
caring 78–9
Chelmsford Mind 92
Chelmsford Prison 72
child care 95
child-derived roles 32

childhood
  problems stemming from 77
  trauma 28
child protection 115, 116, 117, 130, 131, 133
  social worker, support from 48, 62, 63
children
  loss of 47, 59
  safe world for, wish for 88
Children Act (1989) 131, 133, 171
Christianity 80
Church
  as offering most help 95
  support from 48, 62
Classification of Mental and Behavioural Disorders see ICD-10
Clinic for Dissociative Studies 151
Cognitive Analytic Therapy (CAT) 32, 63, 64–5, 67, 90, 114–15, 142, 152, 162, 164
Cognitive Behavioural Therapy (CBT) 32, 64, 113, 115, 164
Colchester 10, 122, 161, 163
Colchester Criminal Justice Mental Health Team, support from 62
Colchester General Hospital 9, 10
Colchester Mind 7, 9, 92
community mental health teams 48, 63
  as offering most help 93–4
  support from 62
community psychiatric nurse (CPN) 83, 93, 94, 115, 116
co-morbidity between Personality Disorder and mental illness 142
compassion 78
Complex Attachment Disorder 27, 39

Complex Post Traumatic Stress Disorder 27, 39
Complex Post Traumatic Syndrome 27–30
confidence 95
confidentiality 52
'congenital delinquency' (Monel) 13
'constitutional inferiority' 13
construct validity 147
Consultation Document (DoH/Home Office, 1999) 16
convictions (prison)
  adult 47, 59
  juvenile 47, 59
co-ordination 85
coping 136
  problems 77, 111
cost-effectiveness 67
counselling 113, 121
counsellors 125
  support from 48, 62, 63
Counter-transference 32
Court Diversion Schemes 129
creativity 80, 96
Criminal Justice Mental Health Team (CJMHT) 48, 62, 129
'Criminal Waste of Life and Time, A' 10
crisis house, support from 48, 62, 85
crisis intervention unit 125
cutting 47, 59, 76, 77, 105

Dangerous Severe Personality Disorder 16, 34, 144, 159, 160, 161, 164
day care 95
day hospital, support from 48
'degenerative deviation' 13
demographics and themes 55–67
dependent (ICD-10 and DSM IV) 18
Department of Health 10, 11, 16, 33, 36,

38, 66, 131, 133, 144, 159, 163, 164, 166
Department of Health and Social Security 133, 166
depression 46, 57, 58, 75–6, 77, 78, 82, 107, 139, 140, 142, 143
desire to hurt others 59
destructiveness 47
   self- 71
determination 79
Detroux, Marc 100
developmental problems 71
diagnosis 9–10, 41, 46, 57
   effect of 127–30
   how users found out about 71–3
   straitjacket of 135–45
Diagnostic and Statistical Manual of Mental Disorders see DSM-I; DSM-III; DSM-IV
Dialectic Behaviour Therapy (DBT) 32–3, 64, 65, 115, 162, 163, 164
diarrhoea 105
Disability Living Allowance (DLA) 74
Disorders of Extreme Stress Not Otherwise Specified (DESNOS) (DSM-IV) 28, 39
'Disassociation' 106–7
disassociation 47, 59, 71
Dissocial Personality Disorder 13, 15, 33, 57, 59, 60, 61, 65, 142
   diagnosis (ICD-10) 17, 41
Dissocial Psychopathic Personality Disorder 46
domestic and employment status 57
drug abuse 47, 59, 76, 77–8
DSM-I 15, 135, 167
DSM-III 28, 135, 136, 167

DSM-IV 9, 15, 16, 17–18, 28, 32, 38, 124, 128, 136, 137, 138, 139, 144, 148, 167

early trauma 29
eating disorder 46, 57, 58, 75, 78
Eating Disorder Centre 92
education 95
Elecroconvulsive Therapy (ECT) 118
emotional abuse, early 47, 61, 100, 110
emotionally unstable borderline type 15 (ICD-10) 17
emotionally unstable impulsive type (ICD-10) 17
employment status 45, 56
   and domestic status 57
endurance/strength 79
'Enduring Personality Change, not Attributable to Brain Damage and Disease' (ICD-10) 28
Essays on the Social Situation of Mental Patients and Other Inmates (Goffman) 127
Essex University 20
ethical approval 52
ethnic origin 45, 55, 96
experiences 59, 99–126
exploitation 47, 59
expressiveness 80

faith, religious 80
family
   as offering most help 89
   support 48, 62, 63
feelings 101–11
   bottled-up 77
First World War 28
foster care 95
friends
   as offering most help 94
   support from 48, 62

gender 45
   and age 56
   comparison of diagnoses 60
general hospital, support from 48, 62
GPs 73, 74, 81, 83, 85, 117, 128
   as offering most help 94
   support from 48, 62, 63
Grendon Underwood Therapeutic Prison 35, 151
Guardian 7, 10
Guardian Angel 109
guilt 76, 138

half-way house 85
hallucinations 75
Hare Psychopathy Checklist 144
'Hate' (poem) 103
Health Authority 7, 153, 155
hearing voices 75, 76, 77, 105–6, 139, 143, 148
'Hedgehog, The' 102
Hell Raiser 106
help: things which have helped most 89–97
   accommodation 95
   advocacy 91
   being away from home area 96
   child care 95
   Church/spiritual beliefs 95
   community mental health teams 93–4
   creativity 96
   education 95
   enough money 96
   ethnic background 96
   family 89
   friends 94
   GPs 94
   hospital 93
   hospital keyworker 93
   incontinence advisor 96
   independence/individuation 95
   medication 91–2

nothing 97
probation officer 96
psychiatrists 93
self 96
self-harm 96
sleeping 96
socialising 96
solicitors 96
therapists 90
voluntary sector 92
helpline 85
Henderson Hospital 7, 16, 36, 42, 66, 74, 83, 90, 114, 145, 153, 156, 163
heroin 76, 77, 78
Histrionic Personality Disorder (ICD-10 and DSM-IV) 18, 57, 58
Holloway Prison 122, 162
holocaust
   survivors 9
   trauma 25–6
home
   area, being way from 96
   and family, wishes for 87
homelessness 77
Home Office 10, 16, 81, 147, 153, 157, 159
   Mental Health Division 150
Home Start 95
homicidal feelings 123
hormone problems 77
hospital 121–2
   keyworker 93
   as offering most help 93
   support from 48, 62, 63
hospitalisation 47, 59
housing 45, 56
'How Do I Cope' (poem) 111
humour, sense of 80

ICD-10 9, 15, 16, 17–18, 28, 32, 38, 124, 128, 136, 137, 138, 139, 148, 168
identity, problems of 70
'I Love My Children' 116–19

imprisonment 47, 59, 61
incontinence advisor 96
independence 87, 95
individuation 95
inferred diagnosis 74
'Inner Child, The' 101
Inner Child Therapy 64, 113, 114, 138
insomnia 76
intelligence 80
International Journal of Social Psychiatry 154
interviews 52–3
invalidating environment 32
isolation 47, 59, 77, 139

James Naylor Foundation 34, 151
Jekyll and Hyde 103
Jesus Christ 95, 109
juvenile convictions 47, 59

Karolinska Psychodynamic Profile 144

labelling 69–70
change in 86–7
laxatives 78
Law Society 161
'Learning Disabilities Secure Unit' 122–3
Life Events and Illness 42
listening 78
'Locked Up' 121–3
loneliness 75
loss of children 47
'Lost Children, The' 100
LSD 77
Lunacy Act (1890) 14, 171

'Mad, Bad or just misunderstood?' (conference) 151
'Mad, Mad, Mad' 104
Marchal, An 100–1
Marchal, Paul 101
Manic Depression 46, 57, 58, 75
manie sans delire (mania without delirium) (Pinel) 13

marital status 45, 56
Masochistic Personality Disorder 136
medication 78, 81, 83, 85
as offering most help 91–2
support from 48, 62, 63
mental alienation 14
Mental Health Care 153
Mental Health Practice 153
Mental Deficiency Act (1913) 14, 15, 171
Mental Health Act (1959) 15, 171
Mental Health Act (1983) 15, 20, 36, 66, 171
Mental Health Act (proposed new) 150, 153, 159–60, 162
Mental Health Review Tribunal 161
Mental Health Services 117
mental health social worker, support from 48, 62
Mental Health Trusts 7, 53, 163
Mind 9, 52, 53, 149
Mind Centre 92
Mind Day Centre 92
'Mommie Dearest' 99–100
money 96
Mood Disorder 13, 58
mood swings 70
moral career of client 127–34
'moral defective' 14
'moral deficiency' 13
'moral imbecility' 13
'moral insanity' (Pritchard) 13
Multiple Personality Disorder 57, 58
Munchausen's Syndrome by Proxy 117, 132
music therapy 113

narcissistic (DSM-IV) 18
National Schizophrenia Fellowship 92
National Homeless Alliance 153

National Institute of Social Work 149
'National Personality Disorder Strategy' 163
National Service Framework for Mental Health (DoH, 1999) 33
neediness, continual 66
neuroses as disorders or diseases 37–9
nightmares 76
'No More Tears' (poem) 109
North East Essex Drug and Alcohol Service (NEEDAS) 93, 113
North Essex Health Authority 10, 161, 170
North Gate Day Centre 94
nurse 74
support from 48, 62

Obsessive Compulsive Disorder (DSM-IV) 18, 46, 57, 58
Obsessive Compulsive Personality Disorder 57, 58
occupation 87
occupational therapist, support from 48, 62, 63, 90
Open Road 92
out of hours help 86
overdosing 47, 59, 76, 77

paedophiles 113
panic
attacks 77, 112
disorder 57, 58, 76, 82
paracetamol 78
paranoia 75, 77
(ICD-10 and DSM-IV) 17
paranoid schizophrenia 20
Paraphilic Rapism 136
parent-derived role 32
parenting help, better 87
Parkhurst Prison 34
patience 79

'Patients Psychiatrists Dislike, The' (Lewis and Appleby) 19
Pedagogy of the Oppressed (Freire) 42
personality
change 70
development 23–6, 71
Personality Disorder 11
Antisocial 15, 33, 136, 142, 144
Assessment Schedule (ICD 10) 144
bad treatment as result of diagnosis 81–2
Borderline 15, 31, 32, 33, 46, 57, 59, 60, 61, 65, 142
Dangerous Severe 16, 34, 144, 159, 160, 164
demographics and themes 55–67
diagnosis 9–10, 41, 46, 57
and disliked patient 19–21
Dissocial 13, 15, 33, 57, 59, 60, 61, 65
Dissocial Psychopathic 46
experiences 59, 99–126
Group 156
history 13–18
Histrionic 57, 58
Masochistic 136
meaning of to service users 69–97
mixed/improved treatment as result of diagnosis 82–3
Multiple 57, 58
Obsessive Compulsive 57, 58
Questionnaire 44
Research Training Programme 49
service users (researchers) 41, 51
Severe 10, 16, 20, 35, 144, 145, 160

subclassifications
16, 17–18
treatability 31–6
Unspecified 57
*Personality Disorder North
Essex News* 157
'Personality Disorder,
who is responsible?'
(conference, 1999)
147
police 81
picked up by 84
support from 48,
62, 63
post natal depression
57, 58, 76, 77
Post Traumatic Stress
Disorder 27, 29, 46,
57, 58
poverty 77
'Predators' (*Panorama*)
34
Premenstrual Dysphoric
Disorder 136
'primal wound' 25
prison 121–2
different treatment
in 84
probation officers 96
Psychiatric Bulletin 153
psychiatrists 71–3, 81,
115, 128
as offering most
help 93
support from 48,
62, 63
psychoanalysis 164
psychologist 90,
114–15
Psychopathic Disorder
15
'psychopathic
inferiority' (Koch) 14
'psychopathic
personality'
(Kraepelin) 14, 15
Psychopathic States
(Henderson) 14
'psychopathic states'
(Koch and Kraepelin)
14
psychopathy 14, 15
psychosis 75
psychotherapists,
support from 48, 62,
63
psychotherapy 85, 113,
115

'Public Protection'
(conference, 1999)
147, 150

Quakers 151

Rampton Special
Hospital 35, 150,
160
'Razor Sharp' 120–1
reciprocal roles 32
reflections and
suggestions 123–6
'Reforming the Mental
Health Act' 159
Reid vs Secretary of
State for Scotland 15,
171
rejection 139
fear of 77
from services 47, 59
relationship difficulties
47, 59, 71, 75
religious beliefs 80
reports and records,
giving diagnosis 73
researchers (service
users) 41, 51
demographics and
themes 55–67
meaning of Person-
ality Disorder to
69–97
Research Ethics
Committee 51
Research Training
Programme,
Personality Disorder
49
'Reunion, The' 100
revictimisation 63
Royal College of
Nursing 153
Royal College of
Psychiatrists 35, 150,
160–1, 171
General Adult Facil-
ity 160
Royal College of
Surgeons 150
Royal Commission on
the Care and Control
of the Feeble Minded
(1904) 14
Royal Edinburgh
Hospital 93
Russell, Lin 160
Russell, Shaun 160

safe house, support from
48, 62, 85, 87
safe world for children,
wish for 88
schizoid (ICD-10 and
DSM-IV) 17
schizophrenia 13, 21,
46, 57, 58, 75
schizotypal (ICD-10
and DSM-IV) 17
Scotland 15
second chance, wish for
88
Second World War 15,
153
'sectioned' 47, 59, 115,
123
security, lack of 77
self 96
-blame 76, 138
-destructiveness 71,
123, 139
distorted sense of
142
-esteem, low 75, 76,
78, 139, 140,
142
-harm 47, 59, 61,
66, 75, 76, 77,
81, 82, 85, 96,
105, 136–7, 140
-help groups 92
sense of 25
sense of humour 80
separate (disassociated)
47, 59
Separation Anxiety 24
service users *see*
researchers (service
users)
Severe Personality
Disorder 10, 16, 20,
35, 144, 145, 160
sexual abuse, early 47,
59, 76, 99–101,
113, 143
sexual problems 75, 77
'Silence' 106
sleeping 96
problems 75
socialising 96
*Social Origins of
Depression* (Brown
and Harris) 42
Social Services 74, 116,
117, 118, 132, 133
bad treatment by 83,
87

social workers 74, 92,
93, 94, 116, 130
solicitors 96
support from 48,
62, 63
South London and
Maudsley NHS Trust
152
Special Hospitals 122,
150
spiritual beliefs
as offering most
help 95
support from 48, 62
*Statistical Manual for the
Use of Institutions for
the Insane* 135
stimulation 87
Stone, Michael 160
strengths of users
78–80
stress 76, 77
stubbornness 79
substance misuse 77–8,
112
suffering as disorder or
disease 37–9
suicidality 61, 107
suicide attempts 47, 59,
66, 108–9
support 48
good 84
group 112
percentage compari-
son of 62
workers 93
supported housing 48,
62, 95

tenacity 79
themes
and demographics
55–67
percentage analysis
of selected 61
Therapeutic
Communities 36,
164
support from 48,
62, 63
therapists, as offering
most help 89
therapy, experience of
112–14
Thompson, Robert
33–4
tiredness 75
'To Whom It May
Concern' 102

tranquillisers 92, 112
Transference 32
'Transgenerational
    Transmission of
    Holocaust Trauma'
    (Fonagy) 25
traumas 76
treatability 31–6
treatment as result of
    diagnosis
        bad 81–2
        by Social
            Services 83
        caused by self 84
        different in prison
            84
        good support 84
        mixed/improved
            82–3
        no difference 83
        not sure 84

'unborn criminal'
    (Lambroso) 13
Unspecified Personality
    Disorder 57
urban alienation, wish
    for less 88

Venables, Jon 34
'Very Confused Poem,
    A' 103
violence 34, 47, 59, 59,
    61, 76
voices, hearing 75, 76,
    77, 105–6, 139,
    143, 148
voluntary centres 53
    support from 48, 62
voluntary sector 53
    as offering most
        help 92
vomiting 105
vulnerability 75

What Works for Whom?
    (Roth and
    Fonagy) 64
Whitemore Prison 35,
    150, 160
will power 79
Winterbourne
    Therapeutic
    Community Day
    Centre 151, 163
'Wise Judge, The'
    118–19
wishes regarding
    treatment and

services in ideal
    world 85–8
    activities/occupa-
        tion 87
    better parenting
        help 87
    better service re-
        sponse 85–6
    don't know 88
    home and family 87
    label changed or re-
        sponded to dif-
        ferently 86–7
    less urban alienation
        88
    not to need services
        88
    out of hours/safe
        house/helpline
        86
    safe world for chil-
        dren 88
    second chance 88
'Woman Falls Down
    Cliff Face' 108–9
work training 87

Author Index

Acland, J. 7, 28, 38,
    165
Adams, R. 7, 156
Adshead, G. 7, 151
Ainscough, C. 27, 165
Aldgate, J. 165
Allen, L. 7, 10, 149,
    150, 151, 153, 155,
    157, 163, 165, 166
Ambrose, M. 168
Appleby, L. 19, 153,
    169

Bateman, A. 65, 163,
    165
Beeforth, M. 11, 165
Bell, E. 19, 165
Bender, L. 24, 165
Beresford, P. 149
Bevan, A. 38
Bevan, P. 153
Blair, T. 11
Bowlby, J. 24, 25, 66,
    133, 145, 165
Boyle, M. 150
Bracken, P. 37, 143,
    165
Bradshaw, J. 127, 165
Brandon, D. 11, 166
Britton, P. 34, 166
Brown, G. 42, 166
Burlingham, D. 24, 166

Cameron 163
Campbell, D. 21, 167
Carvel, J. 160, 166
Cassidy, J. 26, 169
Castillo, A. 7
Castillo, H. 49, 153,
    154, 166, 170
Christiansen, K. 136,
    177
Clark, L. 144, 166
Cleckley, H. 14, 166
Clements, J. 149
Clift, I. 15, 166
Coid, J. 38, 166
Conlan, E. 11, 165
Coulter, J. 148, 166
Cox, J. 161
Coxhead, N. 7, 149,
    153, 166

Dale, C. 35, 171
Davis, E. 147
Diggins, M. 133, 167
Dolan, B. 29, 36, 66,
    167, 169
Duggan, C. 151
Dunn, M. 19, 28, 63,
    167
Durkheim, E. 37, 167

Eastman, N. 35, 167
Escher, S. 148, 171
Esterson, A. 20, 169
Evans, C. 36, 41, 167
Eysenck, H. 144, 167

Fahey, T. 163
Fain, S. 167
Fainman, D. 16
Fenelon, F. 33, 167
Fennel, P. 150
Fisher, M. 41, 167
Fonagy, P. 25, 26, 29,
    31, 33, 64, 65, 133,
    145, 167, 171
Ford, R. 171
Frankl, V. 9, 167
Fransella, F. 148, 167
Freire, P. 42, 149, 167
Freud, A. 24, 166
Freud, S. 13, 20, 37,
    149, 167
Furness, R. 11

Gath, D. 13, 16, 167,
    169, 170
Gawith, L. 171
Gelder, M. 13, 16, 167,
    169, 170
Gilburt, H. 7
Giles, T. 31, 167
Gillan, A. 21, 167
Glasgow, D. 35, 168
Goffman, I. 127, 128,
    130, 168
Gostin, L. 19, 168
Grayley, R. 11, 165
Grove 19
Gustavasson, J. 144,
    172
Guy, S. 35, 168

Haigh, R. 151, 163,
    164
Hare, R. 144, 168
Hargreaves, R. 24, 168
Harris, T. 42, 166
Henderson, D. 14, 168

Herman, J. 27, 29, 59, 168
Heron, J. 42, 168
Hinshelwood, R. 20, 168
Hogue, T. 150
Hooper, A. 163
Hume, A. 35, 168
Hunt, J. 131, 133, 168

Jackson, C. 153
Joan of Arc 14
Johnson, P. 160, 168
Johnson, R. 34—5, 151, 168
Johnson, S. 151
Jordan, C. 168
Joseph, C.S. 27, 168
Julian 151, 156

Kaplan, W. 26, 169
Karen 7, 149, 151, 155
Kellman, H. 144, 170
Kelly, G. 148, 168
Kelly, L. 7, 149, 150, 156
Kernberg, O. 16, 169
Kerr, I. 152, 153
Kiehn, D. 65, 169
Kirk, S. 135, 169
Klein, M. 23, 169
Koch 14, 169
Kraepelin 14, 169
Kutchins, H. 135, 169

Laing, R.D. 20, 23, 169
Laingen, B. 51
Lambroso, C. 13
Lawrence, T.E. 14
Lewis, G. 19, 169
Linehan, M. 32, 33, 65, 142, 169
Linley, P. 171
Liveseley, W. 144, 166

McCann, R. 19, 165
McGauley, G. 38, 170
McKenna, R. 7
Main, M. 26, 169
Marchal, P. 101
Mary Ann 151, 163
Maudsley, H. 13, 169
Mayou, R. 13, 16, 167, 169, 170
Meichenbaum, D. 169
Menzies, D. 36, 169
Merton, R. 37, 169
Moller, C. 160, 161, 162, 169

Monel 13
Morant, N. 7, 42, 49, 153, 154, 170
Morris, M. 35, 169
Morrison, J. 58, 169

National Committee for Mental Hygiene 135, 169
Nemiah, J. 29, 170
Norton, K. 16, 29, 36, 38, 66, 167, 169, 170

Oats, P. 144, 164, 170
O'Keeffe, M. 153
Oldham, J. 19, 30, 38, 144, 170
Oldman, J. 33, 169
Oliver, M. 41, 170
Ooi, R. 38, 170

Parks, P. 64, 170
Parry, G. 19, 28, 63, 167
Pilgrim 128, 147—8, 170
Pinel, P. 13, 170
Pretzer, J. 31, 32, 170
Prins, H. 60, 170
Pritchard 13, 170

Ramon, S. 7, 11, 21, 42, 43, 49, 52, 147, 149, 153, 154, 170
Reber, A. 37, 170
Reed Report 129, 171
Rilke, R.M. 155, 171
Romme, M. 148, 171
Rooke, J. 7
Rose, D. 11, 171
Rossel, R. 144, 172
Roth, A. 31, 33, 64, 171
Rowe, D. 135, 171
Rutter, M. 136, 145, 171
Ryle, A. 32, 33, 65, 152, 171

Scanlon, C. 153
Schneider, K. 14, 171
Schreiber, F. 26, 171
Shorter, E. 15, 135, 171
Silk, K. 33, 169
Skodol, A. 144, 170

Sinasson, V. 151
Smith, J. 160
Smith, S. 16, 170
Snowden, P. 150
Stein, H. 16, 172
Stone, M. 28, 171
Storey, L. 35, 171
Swales, M. 65, 169
Szasz, T. 37, 171

Tallis, D. 7, 10, 49, 171
Thomas, P. 37, 143, 165
Toon, K. 27, 165
Tunstill, J. 165
Turner, R. 31, 171
Tyrer, P. 16, 135, 136, 142, 145, 163, 172

Van der Kolk, B. 29, 30, 31, 59, 142, 143, 168, 172
Verrier, N. 24, 172

Wallcraft, J. 149
Ward, L. 160, 166
Warner, K. 7, 157, 172
Warren, F. 66, 167
Webster, P.F. 167
Weinryb, R. 144, 172
White, C. 7
Whiteley, S. 36, 172
Whittaker, A. 7
Williams, R. 27, 168
Wilson, J. 36, 167

Yarnell, H. 24, 165
Yule, W. 27, 168

Zigmond, T. 160
Zueleta, F. de 27, 152, 172